# Living Here and Hereafter

## Msgr. David E. Rosage

LIVING FLAME PRESS

Cover: Robert Manning

All scripture quotations are from New American Bible

*Nihil Obstat:* Rev. Armand M. Nigro, S.J., *Censor Librorum,*
June 1, 1982

*Imprimatur:* Most Rev. Lawrence H. Welsh, Bishop of
Spokane, June 1, 1982

ISBN: 0-914544-44-6

Printed in the United States of America

# Introduction

Most of us live with a fear and horror of death. We have created a new vocabulary to disguise the reality of death. We speak of a person's "passing" or "being laid to rest."

Some fear can be beneficial and praiseworthy. However, for some the fear of death has become an obsession; for others, almost paralyzing. It is natural to fear the unknown. Death carries with it a great finality; there is no turning back, no second chance.

In our times, as nuclear destruction threatens us with annihilation, we are searching for the meaningfulness of life. We are striving to learn what life after death is like. This desire has flooded our markets with apocalyptic literature that furthers our curiosity but sheds no clear light.

Jesus speaks of his own death as his glorification. He wants us to see our own death as our going through the doorway of life leading to our own glorification. Jesus did not come to give us a detailed description of life hereafter. He came to teach us how to live in order to attain the eternal life awaiting us.

Life is a journey toward our heavenly home.

This journey begins at the moment of our birth. It is also the beginning of our death. Our span of life is a temporary sojourn in this land of exile, conditioning us and preparing us to enter eternal life.

Our preparation consists primarily in our dying to our own self-centeredness. As we do so, we are making ourselves more and more receptive to the influx of God's divine life. This process is a lifetime struggle. However, the moment of death affords us a golden opportunity to make the final oblation of ourselves into the hands of our loving Father.

With this final and total giving of ourselves to God, the Trinitarian life shared with us in Baptism bursts into full fruition.

LIVING HERE AND HEREAFTER offers some prayerful reflections for each day of the month as a humble attempt to assuage our fear of death and assist us in the process of giving ourselves totally to God by dying the little deaths of each day.

Above all, it is a feeble attempt to make us more and more aware of the Father of Infinite Love awaiting the moment when he may receive us into his arms and fill us with that love that knows no bounds.

As we prayerfully listen to the Lord speaking to us in his Word, we will begin to experience the love, peace and joy which are a foretaste of the eternal happiness which awaits us.

# **Table of Contents**

# 1 God's Love

## "As the Father has loved me, so I have loved you." John 15:9

One of the most basic truths which we are challenged to face and accept is that God loves us. He is the gracious Father who loves us just as we are. He is our Abba.

God created us as an expression of his love. He provides for our every need at every moment of every day. Every heartbeat is a proof of his providential love.

His forgiving, healing love brings us back to him if we stray away from him. His love is enduring. It never changes, regardless of what we do.

This overwhelming love of the Lord for us personally and individually is a mystery, difficult for us to accept because our thinking is so earthly, so conceptual. God's infinite love for us cannot be grasped with our finite minds. We look at various facets of his love to penetrate at least partially its great mystery.

St. John's brief statement speaks volumes to us:

"Yes, God so loved the world that he gave his only Son, that whoever believes in him

may not die but may have eternal life."
*(John 3:16)*

What boundless love is revealed in that one short sentence! What more reassurance do we need that we are lovable and loved?

Genuine, mature love gives graciously, willingly and without counting the cost. What greater gift could God have given us than himself in the person of Jesus? Listen to the Father asking you through his prophet, Isaiah: "What more was there to do for my vineyard that I had not done?" *(5:4)*.

The more frequently and deeply we contemplate this mystery of God's boundless love for us, the greater will be our joy and the more generous will be our response in love.

Jesus came into the world to manifest the love of the Father and his own love for us in a very realistic and concrete way.

"As the Father has loved me, so I have loved you" *(John 15:9)*. The Father's love for Jesus is infinite. It cannot be any greater. Jesus assures us that he loves us with that same infinite love. His love for us never changes, regardless of what we have done. It is without limit. It is unconditional.

Jesus proved his love by reaching out in loving concern for everyone. He respected all persons — saint and sinner, young and old, Jew and Gentile. Jesus was always aware that every person is called to be a son or daughter of his Father — his own brothers and sisters.

Jesus' love touched all those who were in

need — the suffering, the broken, the dying. He healed people, not so much to prove his divine power as to manifest his love for the poor, the downtrodden, the weak, those in pain and sorrow.

To the widow of Naim he said: "Do not cry." Then he raised her son and gave him back to her *(Luke 7:11ff)*. The leper pleaded hesitantly: "Lord, if you will to do so, you can cure me." Try to fathom the depths of the love which prompted Jesus to reply: "I do will it. Be cured" *(Luke 5:12ff)*.

To the paralytic Jesus said: "My son, your sins are forgiven" *(Mark 2:5)*. And to Jairus: "Fear is useless; what is needed is trust and her life will be spared" *(Luke 8:50)*.

Jesus' love is also human. The evangelist tells us: "Jesus loved Martha and her sister and Lazarus very much" *(John 11:5)*. Jesus' love for these friends was quite apparent to the Jews. At the tomb of Lazarus, "Jesus began to weep, which caused the Jews to remark, 'See how much he loved him!'" *(John 11:35ff)*.

Jesus loves us with the same love with which he loved not only Martha, Mary and Lazarus but also the widow of Naim, the paralytic, the leper and every other person. We are precious to him.

Jesus assures us that it was his love which motivated him to come into the world to lay down his life for us. "I came that they might have life and have it to the full." Further:

"For these sheep I will give my life. The Father loves me for this: that I lay down my life to take it up again. No one takes it from me; I lay it down freely." (John 10:10, 15, 17-18)

The intensity of Jesus' love was revealed when he said in his Last Discourse in the Upper Room:

"There is no greater love than this: to lay down one's life for one's friends." (John 15:13)

We are his friends. The next day Jesus proved his love by laying down his life for us.

## "I will dwell with them and walk among them." 2 Corinthians 6:16

The love which Jesus has for each one of us goes far beyond laying down his life for us. Love seeks closeness to the beloved. Love wants to be a part of the life of the person loved.

Jesus loves us so much he chose not to leave us alone in this land of exile. He wanted to remain with us, to encourage us, to accompany us, to love us:

> "I will not leave you orphaned; I will come back to you." *(John 14:18)*

In that same Discourse Jesus prays for our unity with him and with our brothers and sisters. He does not force himself upon us. He wants us to be receptive to receive his love. He prays for us to his Father for this special gift of openness:

> "That they may be one, even as we are one . . . That they may be one as you, Father, are in me, and I in you; I pray that they may be one in us." *(John 17:11 & 21)*

He cannot separate himself from us. In his parting words, he gives us the reassurance of his love.

What could speak to us more eloquently of the fathomless love of Jesus than his final words in Matthew's Gospel:

"And know that I am with you always, until the end of the world." *(Matthew 28:20)*

How does Jesus remain with us? There are many different kinds of presences in our human relations. During a long-distance phone call we are present to another person even though we are separated by many miles. We could be traveling in the same airplane and be physically present to one of our close friends and yet be totally unaware of our proximity to each other. If we are listening to a speaker, he becomes more present to us than we are to him. We know his thoughts as he speaks, but he does not know ours as we listen. That can be a blessing at times!

The Bishops in Vatican Council II taught that Jesus is present in the world in many different ways. He is present in his Word, in the Eucharist, in his Body the Church and in each one of us.

At the time of our Baptism, the Father invited us to become members of his family. He adopted us as his sons and daughters; he shared with us the tremendous gift of his own divine life. From that moment on we became the temples of the Holy Spirit. St. Paul reiterates this truth many times, hoping that we might never be oblivious to our true dignity.

Jesus promised that the Holy Spirit would abide with us and within us:

> "I will ask the Father and he will give you another Paraclete — to be with you always . . . he remains with you and will be within you." (John 14:16)

Saint Paul asks:

> "Are you not aware that you are the temple of God, and that the Spirit of God dwells in you? If anyone destroys God's temple, God will destroy him. For the temple of God is holy, and you are that temple." (1 Corinthians 3:16)

Saint Paul repeats emphatically:

> "You must know that your body is a temple of the Holy Spirit, who is within — the Spirit you have received from God. You are not your own. You have been purchased at a price. So glorify God in your body." (1 Corinthians 6:19)

And again the astounding good news:

> "You are the temple of the living God, just as God has said: 'I will dwell with them and walk among them. I will be their God and they shall be my people . . . I will welcome you and be a father to you and you will be my sons and daughters.'" (2 Corinthians 6:16ff)

This is so incomprehensible that Jesus speaks of it by means of a simple allegory: "I am the vine, you are the branches. . . ." *(John 15:1-8).*

The vine and the branches are of one plant. It is hard to distinguish where the vine ends and the branch begins. The branch is useless, dead, unless it stays attached to the vine for its life-giving nourishment.

God's goodness is reflected in this allegory. God lets us, the branches, blossom and bear fruit. It would be impossible without his life-giving presence.

We have been baptized into Trinitarian life. Since the Lord is present in us as in his temple, our resurrection has already begun. He is more present to us than the oxygen we inhale to sustain life; more present than the blood circulating through our veins.

Jesus promised that he would remain with us always. This means that he will also be very present at the moment of our death. He will take us by the hand and welcome us into his kingdom.

With Jesus living in us, our resurrection has already begun. It will reach its fullness at the moment of death.

## THREE

# "No one who comes will I ever reject."
**John 6:37**

By its very nature friendship is mutual. Love seeks to receive love in return. When we are aware that we are loved, we want to respond to that love. Love gives and acts.

In the awareness of God's overwhelming love for us, we ask with the psalmist:

"How shall I make a return to the Lord for all the good he has done for me?" *(Psalm 116:12)*

All that Jesus asks, for the outpouring of his love upon us, is our love in return. He asks us the same question he asked Simon Peter on the shore of the Lake of Galilee after his resurrection: "Simon, son of John, do you love me?" *(John 21:15)*.

He asked that question of Peter three times. Peter realized that his love was imperfect but that he was trying to love Jesus. That is all Jesus wanted. He wanted Peter to realize that if he were trying to love, then Jesus was happy, because desire is all we can accomplish sometimes. And that of itself is gift.

After the third query, Peter responded:

"Lord, you know everything. You know well that I love you." *(John 21:15ff)*

We might respond to Jesus in much the same way when he asks us if we love him:

"Yes, Lord, you know everything. You know that we want to love you, but easily we forget. We take your love for granted. You know how self-centered we are at times. But, Lord, we are trying, and we know this pleases you."

All that Jesus asks is our good will. Are we trying to love him? Jesus explains to us *how* we can love him:

"He who obeys the commandments he has from me is the man who loves me; and he who loves me will be loved by my Father. I too will love him and reveal myself to him." *(John 14:21)*

Keeping the commandments means more than simply avoiding sin by following the prohibitions of the Ten Commandments. It means living according to the Way which Jesus outlined for us, especially in his law of love of God and neighbor. In doing so, we must have the dispositions which Jesus mapped out for us in the Beatitudes.

Life is a continual dying to self and a surrendering more and more to God. Numerous ways present themselves each day for us to die to self: a kind word spoken to a person; refraining from retorting sharply to another; giving our time and attention to someone who may importune us at the time; accepting the infirmities and afflictions of old age; spending some time with the Lord each day listening to what he is speaking to our hearts. These are but a few of the myriad ways of saying "yes" to God and "no" to self.

We express our love for the Lord by trusting him. When we love people, we trust them. Jesus asks for a loving trust in him:

> "Do not let your hearts be troubled. Have faith in God and faith in me. In my Father's house there are many dwelling places; otherwise, how could I have told you that I was going to prepare a place for you? I am indeed going to prepare a place for you, and then I shall come back to take you with me, that where I am you also may be." *(John 14:1ff)*

What love these words express! Jesus loves us so much he wants us to be with him in the bliss of heaven for all eternity. What reassurance and encouragement Jesus gives us when he promises us that he will come back to take us with him! How can we doubt his love?

Jesus also prays to the Father for us and for our eternal union with him. The prayer of Jesus is always answered. May his petition find a home in our hearts:

"Father, all those you gave me I would
have in my company where I am, to see
this glory of mine which is your gift to me,
because of the love you bore me before
the world began." *(John 17:24)*

An outpouring of love for us is spoken in this
prayer.

Earlier, Jesus enkindled our hope and guaran-
teed our happiness, saying:

"All that the Father gives me shall come
to me; no one who comes will I ever
reject." *(John 6:37)*

Joy, happiness, comfort and consolation are
promises of Jesus to us as we journey toward our
eternal destiny. They leave no room for doubt or
fear. "Come, Lord Jesus!" *(Revelation 22:20)*.

# 2 Privileged Suffering

**"If only we suffer with him so as to be glorified with him."** Romans 8:17

Suffering is the lot of every human being and it still remains a mystery. It has baffled us from time immemorial. Who can understand it?

We have adopted many different attitudes toward pain and suffering, so pervasive in our lives. Some think that suffering must be endured stoically, since we cannot avoid it. Some look on it as a punishment for sin. They recall the words of Genesis when Adam and Eve were expelled from the Garden: "By the sweat of your face shall you get bread to eat" *(Genesis 3:19)*.

There is, however, another view. Jesus came into this world to give us a new vision, and a new meaning to suffering. He was himself "a man of sorrows." Saint Paul reminds us: "But if we are children (of God), we are heirs as well: heirs of God, heirs with Christ, if only we suffer with him so as to be glorified with him" *(Romans 8:17)*.

If we are willing to give ourselves totally to the Father's will as Jesus did, if we are willing to suffer along with Jesus, we shall also be glorified with him.

We Christians have been baptized into Trinitarian life, and we are the temples in which the Trinity now dwells. This indwelling underpins the meaning of suffering and death.

We have an extraordinary power within us, from the presence of the triune God dwelling in us. God wishes to make us participators in his own divine life: "Sharers of the divine nature" (2 Peter 1:4). Saint Irenaeus says that "God became man so that man might become divine."

We must undergo some purifying suffering and do some dying to self to be receptive to the influx of his divine life. For example: the more we drain out liquid from the faucet at the bottom of a container, the more can be poured into the top. If the container is completely drained, it can be filled anew with fresh liquid. As we are emptied more and more of our self-interests, the more God will be able to fill us with the living waters of his divine life.

God's loving presence and power within us is a mystery which leads us beyond the cross on to the resurrection. A strong dynamic faith, a persevering hope and an enduring love enable us to rise above the natural and be more open to God's life operative within us.

Suffering is a part of our whole life's span, from birth until death. Suffering is physical, psychological and spiritual. Whatever the source and cause of our sufferings, growth and maturity can come from them, detaching us and enabling us to give ourselves more generously to our Father.

Sickness, pain, infirmities and limitations of our human nature and old age are physical. Fears, anxieties, worries and hurts which arise out of our humanness and sinfulness are psychological.

Laboring at the sweat of our brow for our daily bread can be another form of suffering. Work can be monotonous and routine. It can be fatiguing and exhausting. The divine indwelling affords us a broader vision — to see our labor as sharing in the creative power of God, bringing the world to a higher state of perfection. It is also an ideal way of reaching out in love to others, since our work benefits them.

Yet one of the greatest sources of suffering is love. Human love should be the greatest and most pleasant source of our happiness. However, to love unselfishly means a continual dying to self. Love is always vulnerable. Love is always an invitation to suffer.

To love means to give, to let go. To say "yes" to another requires overcoming our own selfishness. We cannot give unselfishly unless we love. In this dying to self are joy and happiness. There can also be much pain. This is the mystery of love.

No one suffered as much as Jesus because no other person ever loved as intensely as he did. No other person ever gave of self as completely as Jesus did.

If we want to love God, we must abandon ourselves completely to him and permit him to do whatever he wishes.

Jesus prepares us for suffering and encourages us:

> "I tell you truly: you will weep and mourn while the world rejoices; you will grieve for a time, but your grief will be turned to joy." *(John 16:20)*

Saint Paul praises God for suffering and encourages us to do the same:

> "Praised be God, the Father of our Lord Jesus Christ, the Father of mercies, and the God of all consolation! He comforts us in all our afflictions and thus enables us to comfort those who are in trouble, with the same consolation we have received from him. As we have shared much in the suffering of Christ, so through Christ do we share abundantly in his consolation." *(2 Corinthians 1:3ff)*

# "If we have died with Christ, we believe that we are also to live with him."

**Romans 6:8**

Suffering of any kind is a sort of dying to ourselves, to our own egoism, in order that Jesus can become the Lord and Master of our lives. At Baptism we committed ourselves to the Lord. To live out our commitment we must die to our self-centeredness each day. As we die to ourselves we will experience a new union with the indwelling Lord:

> "Be intent on things above rather than on things of earth. After all, you have died! Your life is hidden now with Christ in God. When Christ our life appears, then you shall appear with him in glory." *(Colossians 3:2ff)*

Jesus tells us that, after we have been empowered by the Holy Spirit, we are to become his witnesses to the world. We witness more powerfully to our faith and hope in life after death, not by our attitudes and reactions on our deathbed but rather by living with a cheerful acceptance of the sufferings which may come our way.

Suffering yields many fruits. It raises our focus above the mundane, to eternity. It helps us detach ourselves from temporal preoccupations. It also detaches us from our own disordered will and desires.

Experience teaches us how detaching suffering can be. For example, a person who is goal-oriented and well-programmed will be quite impatient and unhappy with anyone or anything which causes him or her any deviation from well-laid plans. However, serious illness or other problems can cause loss of interest in many of the things which previously seemed to be vitally important.

Similarly, as we mature in life, the types of recreation and entertainment of former years may no longer hold interest for us. Suffering has a similar effect in other areas of our lives.

Saint Paul puts it this way:

> "Those things I used to consider gain I have now reappraised as loss in the light of Christ. I have come to rate all as loss in the light of the surpassing knowledge of my Lord Jesus Christ. For his sake I have forfeited everything; I have accounted all else rubbish so that Christ may be my wealth and I may be in him." *(Philippians 3:7ff)*

One of the fruits of suffering will be this same transforming effect in our lives. Many of the things we thought important will lose their glitter.

We will become more God-centered, our focus more heavenward.

Jesus conquered sin and death so that we could be reunited with him forever. As we become more aware of this, our lives on this earth, especially at the moment of our death, will reflect a joy, a radiance, a peace which the world cannot give. Christians should give witness to the world of what genuine happiness is all about. Our pragmatic world measures happiness and success mainly in terms of power and pleasure.

Our faith assures us that Jesus conquered death; death, then, is but a doorway into a fuller, richer life with him.

Jesus is dwelling within us. He comes to us with that same power which enabled him to overcome sin and death:

> "I came that they might have life and have it to the full." *(John 10:10)*

Since Jesus is dwelling in us, we can say to the many little deaths of each day and to the final death we must undergo:

> "Where are your plagues, O death! where is your sting, O nether world!" *(Hosea 13:14)*

Saint Paul had experienced with joy the saving power of Jesus long before he faced final death at the time of his martyrdom. "I face death every day" *(1 Corinthians 15:31)*.

"When the corruptible frame takes on incorruptibility and the mortal immortality, then will the saying of scripture be fulfilled: 'Death is swallowed up in victory.' 'O death, where is your victory? O death, where is your sting?' The sting of death is sin, and sin gets its power from the law. But thanks be to God who has given us the victory through our Lord Jesus Christ." (1 Corinthians 15:54ff)

As we learn to die to selfishness each day, our union with the Trinity will be deepened so that nothing will be able to separate us from the love of God. As this conviction is strengthened, we enjoy a peace and certitude that death leads into final and total union with God.

Even before death, we are already sharing in the resurrection of Jesus. In Baptism we become living members of his Body, and the Holy Spirit lives within us. How true are the words of Saint Paul:

"If the Spirit of him who raised Jesus from the dead dwells in you, then he who raised Jesus from the dead will bring your mortal bodies to life also, through his Spirit dwelling in you." (Romans 8:11)

The Holy Spirit dwells in us. We are his temples. He is constantly enlightening us to see God's original plan. Gradually we understand how all things fit into God's divine design. Our own knowledge and understanding become "other-worldly."

In this transformation we are less and less concerned about the opinions of those living a worldly life around us. All the events of our daily life are visible in the light of eternity.

The risen Jesus abides with us here and now. He never leaves us; he leads us through the happenings of each day.

The presence within us of Jesus, who has conquered sin and death, enables us to mock death and dispel our fears about death:

> "If we have died with Christ, we believe that we are also to live with him. We know that Christ, once raised from the dead, will never die again; death has no more power over him. His death was death to sin, once for all; his life is life for God. In the same way, you must consider yourselves dead to sin but alive for God in Christ Jesus." *(Romans 6:8ff)*

Suffering remains a mystery. However, in prayer we become more aware of Jesus walking at our side and leading us up the stepping-stones of suffering into eternal union with our loving Father.

## THREE

## "Whoever believes in me, though he should die, will come to life." John 11:26

Most of us are concerned with the wrong questions about death. We want to know when, where and how death will come, and what our bodies will be like in the resurrection. We are anxious, curious and concerned about heaven.

Christians should never be hung up on questions like these. We will never know the answers to these questions in this life. We are living in a time-and-space existence here in this world and there are no adequate comparisons.

Instead, our big concerns ought to be: how can I today, at this very moment, be freed from any fear or anxiety about death? How can I, as a son or daughter of God, trust him more and live in the freedom we should all enjoy?

The only way we are freed from selfishness and death and the false values of the world is to live with the risen, glorified Jesus within us. Jesus wants to take possession of our hearts so that we will live for him alone.

Freedom is the progressive surrender in love to Jesus, so that at every moment of our lives he is Lord. As we do so, fear begins to disappear. Confidence and trust in him increases as love for him grows in our hearts:

"Love has no room for fear; rather, perfect love casts out all fear." *(1 John 4:18)*

Jesus is the power living within us that helps us live every moment of every day as a gift in love to the Father. Every activity, every thought, every word becomes our love-offering to our gracious Father.

This gives us our true dignity. We are loved by God. We are his adopted sons and daughters. This means that we are lovable and loved. This gives us the freedom to love as he loves us. Freedom is one of God's gifts to us; it is that gift of loving ourselves and the entire world as God loves us and loves the world.

Death is the last opportunity for us to surrender ourselves freely and willingly into the loving arms of our heavenly Father.

In spite of the pain, temptation or doubt about a life hereafter, we can cry out with the triumphant Jesus: "Father, into your hands I commend my spirit" *(Luke 23:46)*.

We cannot experience this final moment of victory unless we permit the divine life given us in Baptism to be operative and dynamic. Death and resurrection are something we live each day as the fruit of our baptismal commitment.

By dying to ourselves each day and living for Jesus, we can share progressively in the life of the risen Jesus. We will come to understand better that death is the outpouring of his divine life upon us.

The authentic test of how completely we have truly died in this life — and are already risen in Christ — is how much we live for others:

> "That we have passed from death to life we know because we love the brothers. The man who does not love is among the living dead. Anyone who hates his brother is a murderer, and you know that eternal life abides in no murderer's heart. The way we came to understand love was that he laid down his life for us; we too must lay down our lives for our brothers. I ask you, how can God's love survive in a man who has enough of this world's goods yet closes his heart to his brother when he sees him in need? Little children, let us love in deed and in truth and not merely talk about it." *(1 John 3:14-18)*

Suffering and death are parts of a growth process. This vision is far more complete and comfortable than our usual understanding of death as a separation of the immortal soul from a corruptible body.

Death, as an essential to growth, is well-rooted in Sacred Scripture. It manifests to us that we are whole persons, growing into eternal life through a series of death moments that lead us throughout our entire lives from selfishness into a new freedom as children of God. "Unless the grain of wheat falls to the earth and dies, it remains just a grain of wheat. But if it dies, it produces much fruit" *(John 12:24)*.

We live with this assurance of Jesus: "I solemnly assure you, if a man is true to my word he shall never see death" *(John 8:51)*.

Then John explains how we can be true to the word of Jesus: "The commandment we have from him is this: whoever loves God must also love his brother" *(1 John 4:21)*.

We must prayerfully reflect on this meaning of death. In prayer, God will reveal to us that true life, given us when we love one another, is eternal and that no one can take it away from us.

Death, the wages of sin, has been conquered and transformed by Jesus' redemptive love into the entrance to eternal life.

It has been said that we die as we live. Perhaps it would be more accurate to say that we die as we have loved, since Jesus made love the condition for entering eternal life.

Contemplate both the scene and the words of Jesus at the tomb of Lazarus. See death as a passage into an eternal union of love. Jesus loves us and is anxious for the day when we will be united with him, along with the Father and the Holy Spirit, in a community of perfect love:

> "I am the resurrection and the life: whoever believes in me, though he should die, will come to life; and whoever is alive and believes in me will never die. Do you believe this?" *(John 11:25f)*

# 3 Wages of Sin

## "The wages of sin is death." Romans 6:23

From Sacred Scripture and the constant teaching of the Church, we know that death is the result of sin.

According to God's original plan, we were to live in a peaceful relationship with God and with created nature. By grace, God established a deep, personal relationship with us. Unable to describe fully, this close spiritual relationship between God and us, the sacred writer speaks of God as walking "about (with Adam) in the garden at the breezy time of the day" *(Genesis 3:8)*. This breezy time was the most pleasant time of day and indicates a special relationship.

God set us only one caveat for maintaining this intimate relationship:

> "You are free to eat from any of the trees of the garden except the tree of knowledge of good and bad. From that tree you shall not eat; the moment you eat from it you are surely doomed to die." *(Genesis 2:16f)*

The first humans disregarded God's wishes. They ate forbidden fruit. They refused loving obedience to their God. They said "no" to God. They refused to accept the love of their Creator.

This sin fractured the relationship radically. The result of sin was a breaking of the unity with the Father. This rupture is dramatically described in the Book of Genesis: "The Lord God therefore banished him from the garden of Eden, to till the ground from which he had been taken" *(Genesis 3:23)*.

Sin brought death into the world. Before sin there was no death. If man were to die to reach a higher and fuller union with the Lord God, it would have been more like a sleep rather than the violent upheaval it now is because of sin.

Many think that a peaceful transition from mortal existence into union with God was the kind of death that Mary experienced: a quiet, peaceful sleeping away from this mortal life. In fact, it is often called her dormition — her sleeping.

Saint Paul says flatly: "The wages of sin is death" *(Romans 6:23)*. However, death is not a punishment levied by a vindictive, vengeful God. No, the wages of sin is death because serious sin deliberately severs the living relationship with our loving Father. Death is the final stage of raising our sinful nature to perfect union in love with God.

As a concerned pastor, St. James writes:

"The tug and lure of his own passion tempt every man. Once passion has conceived, it gives birth to sin, and when sin reaches maturity it begets death." *(James 1:14f)*

Saint Paul instructs the Galatians about the wages of sin (recall that all Scripture is written for our instruction, too):

"Make no mistake about it, no one makes a fool of God! A man will reap only what he sows. If he sows in the field of the flesh, he will reap a harvest of corruption; but if his seed-ground is the spirit, he will reap everlasting life." *(Galatians 6:7f)*

The happenings in the Garden of Eden constitute a sad story, but there is a happy ending. Even as God was expelling Adam and Eve from the Garden, he was promising them a Redeemer *(Genesis 3:15)*.

Saint Paul did say: "The wages of sin is death." But he was quick to add: "But the gift of God is eternal life in Christ Jesus our Lord" *(Romans 6:23)*.

The Church, too, takes up the same refrain in the Easter Vigil Proclamation:

"O happy fault,
O necessary sin of Adam,
which gained for us so great a Redeemer!"

## "If we have died with Him we shall also live with Him." 2 Timothy 2:11

Jesus came to teach us how to live and how to die. Jesus taught us not only how to live a happy life in this world, but gave us many reassurances about life hereafter with him. To this end he prayed:

"Father, all those you gave me I would have in my company where I am." *(John 17:24)*

Pondering prayerfully the words of Jesus dispels many fears, doubts and misgivings about death.

Jesus also taught us by his own example how to give ourselves totally to God in love each day, so that death will become the final and total surrender of ourselves in love to our Father. Each dying to self-centeredness and each surrender in love to our Father is another step in giving ourselves completely to him.

We can give ourselves more generously as we acknowledge that Jesus conquered sin and death. His redeeming love helps us scorn death as a punishment and an effect of sin. "Death is swallowed up in victory. O death, where is your victory? O death, where is your sting?" *(1 Corinthians 15:54)*.

To the Romans Paul writes: "The law of the spirit, the spirit of life in Christ Jesus, has freed you from the law of sin and death" *(Romans 8:2)*.

In spite of all of these reassurances, death still seems a punishment for sin. Who of us can say, even though we love God as deeply as we can, that when we face death we will not doubt God's mercy? We can depend on the temptations of the evil one to lead us into doubt, fear and anxiety.

There is such an unknown about death, such darkness, such mystery. This causes all of us some dread and fear because we still regard death as the "wages of sin."

Guided by the Holy Spirit, John reassures us:

"I am writing this to keep you from sin. But if anyone should sin, we have, in the presence of the Father, Jesus Christ, an intercessor who is just. He is an offering for our sins, and not for our sins only, but for those of the whole world." *(1 John 2:1f)*

Jesus not only taught us that our lives should be a total giving of ourselves to God, but he himself lived out that teaching by fulfilling the Father's will perfectly in his daily ministry. He was single-hearted in this respect.

Jesus showed us the way. He healed all who came to him even though he was weary; he blessed little children even when he was exhausted; he gave his full attention and love to blind Bartimaeus even though the crowd demanded Jesus' full attention. These are only a few of the highlights of Jesus' dedication to his ministry. His whole life was a dying to self.

We, too, have daily opportunities to die to self and give ourselves in love to God and to others. This very moment, as we prayerfully ponder these thoughts, we are giving ourselves to God. We are dying to self when we perform a kind deed for another; when we patiently listen; when we smile through our tears; when we visit by phone or in person someone who is lonely or suffering.

This kind of giving is not only a preparation for our final gift of self, but it is the only genuine source of happiness. It brings joy and satisfaction.

We strive to give ourselves freely and completely to God so that he can be the Lord of our lives. Then death will be the climax of a lifetime of choosing God and his preferences.

With Jesus on the cross we say:

"Father, into your hands I commend my spirit."

And Jesus' reply will be the same to us as it was to the thief:

"I assure you: this day you will be with me in paradise." *(Luke 23:43 & 46)*

# 4 Death of Jesus

## "Into your hands I commend my spirit." Psalm 31:6

We Christians understand more about our own inevitable death as we prayerfully consider the death of Jesus. It was his long-awaited hour. "I have a baptism to receive. What anguish I feel till it is over!" *(Luke 12:50).*

Jesus' whole ministry moved toward the cross. On at least three separate occasions he foretold his passion, death and resurrection *(Matthew 16:21ff; 17:22ff; 20:17ff).*

Jesus died on a certain day in time on Calvary's hill outside the walls of the Holy City. However, his death was but the climax of a whole life of giving of and dying to himself. His death was the gift of his entire life: daily dying to himself, to his own self-interests, to his own hopes and ambitions; giving himself in loving surrender to his Father.

His whole life, from his first breath in Bethlehem to his last gasp on the cross, was one continuous gift of himself. "It is not to do my own will that I have come down from heaven, but to do the will of him who sent me" *(John 6:38).*

Each moment of Jesus' earthly life was a preparation for his death. His life was a life of giving. Every choice he made was in freedom to give his every thought, word and deed to his Father in heaven.

In that resolve he prayed in the Garden of Gethsemane: "Father, if it is your will, take this cup from me; yet not my will but yours be done" *(Luke 22:42)*. The next day on the cross he fulfilled this determination to give himself completely into the hands of his Father.

This was not easy for Jesus. It was a difficult struggle for him to give himself completely and unreservedly to his Father's will. Jesus struggled with this temptation throughout his whole earthly sojourn.

The temptations in the desert, the agony in the Garden of Gethsemane and the temptations on the cross manifest something of the inner battle, the inner dying to self, which Jesus endured before he could give himself in loving abandonment to the Father.

He gave himself freely in love by focusing all his thoughts, words and deeds on his Father. From this focus Jesus derived the strength, the courage and the generosity which enabled him to give himself totally to the Father's will.

Mount Tabor manifests this well. Jesus took his prayer team — Peter, James and John — and went up the mountain to pray. At his Baptism the Father had asked Jesus to commit himself to his teaching ministry. On Tabor he was asked to accept the mission of suffering. In prayer Jesus found the strength to say "yes" to the Father. Only after his consent was Jesus transfigured, radiating his glory through his humanity.

Jesus endured and overcame temptations, showing us the way. He was telling us that fear, doubt, depression and even near-despair are part of our human condition. Love urges us to give and enables us to conquer temptations, provided we cry out to Jesus in our struggle. Jesus not only endured struggle but he sanctified it for us.

We struggle daily with the same temptations. We want our freedom, our independence. It is difficult for us to submit to God's will and freely surrender ourselves in loving obedience to the Father. To die to our self-will and to give ourselves freely to God requires love. Once we have experienced the Father's love for us, our giving becomes easier. To give completely is a gift from the Holy Spirit who is the Spirit of Love.

Only in prayer do we touch the mystery of God's love in the death of Jesus. Otherwise we may look upon Jesus' death, his kenosis or pouring out of himself, as some sort of legalistic satisfaction, a means of making atonement for our sins.

This theory could lead us to believe that mankind collectively sinned and contracted a huge debt which we could never repay; and that Jesus as God offered the Father, on our behalf, a complete satisfaction which would cancel our debt. This is beyond the ability of humans to do; hence only Jesus, as God and Man, could satisfy this debt as the Father might demand.

This view makes God vengeful and vindictive, which is not the God of Scripture. This kind of God is inconceivable if we have experienced the Father's love for us.

It is true that Jesus did atone for our sinfulness, but he did much more. He rose from the dead so that he could share his divine life with us. This makes us the temples of the Holy Spirit. We are the adopted sons and daughters of God. Our resurrection has already begun.

We were healed and saved not just at the moment of Jesus' death on Calvary's hill. Jesus is in his glory now. His glory is continuing his redemptive work at every moment of the day. This saving process continues and grows every day in our lives.

With the grace and enlightenment of the Holy Spirit, we are invited to contemplate the mystery of our redemption, to become ever more aware that Jesus is dwelling with us and within us. By his very presence and power he is aiding us in the process of yielding more completely to the Father's will.

Traffic "yield" signs on the street should remind us to yield to our loving Father.

We make Paul's words our own:

"I have been crucified with Christ, and the life I live now is not my own; Christ is living in me. I still live my human life, but it is a life of faith in the Son of God, who loved me and gave himself for me." *(Galatians 2:19f)*

## "Whoever loses his life for my sake will find it." Matthew 16:25

Jesus was not a helpless victim of the atrocities of his enemies. He was not merely passive during his death ordeal. That would have been murder, not sacrifice. On the contrary, Jesus freely gave himself as an oblation. Listen to his own words:

> "The Father loves me for this: that I lay down my life to take it up again. No one takes it from me; I lay it down freely. I have power to lay it down, and I have power to take it up again. This command I received from my Father." (John 10:17f)

This selfless submission, this generous giving of Jesus pleased the Father. When we follow Jesus as his disciples and identify with him even in offering our lives to the Father, this also pleases the Father, who welcomes us into fuller, richer life in union with him.

Jesus willingly and freely became human. By his Incarnation he identified with all humanity. Jesus chose to accept the suffering and dying of every human being. He freely willed to drink the bitter chalice of suffering which every man and woman must endure. He wished to become poor with the poor and lonely with the lonely, especially the abandoned and unloved.

The death of Jesus is a model for all Christians who face death. Jesus reached his full potential as Savior and Redeemer as he freely surrendered his life to the Father.

Jesus suffered physical pain as any one of us do. On the cross he suffered as any other human being would in crucifixion.

On the cross Jesus brought together his whole lifetime of willingly and gladly giving and surrendering himself in love to the Father.

Nowhere did Jesus give himself so completely to the Father as on the cross. There his oblation reached its climax. Such total giving could be accomplished only through love.

The secret of peaceful resignation to death for the Christian lies in the power of the cross. It is a wisdom beyond human comprehension:

> "The message of the cross is complete absurdity to those who are headed for ruin, but to us who are experiencing salvation, it is the power of God. . . . For God's folly is wiser than men, and his weakness more powerful than men." *(1 Corinthians 1:18 & 25)*

We Christians are both spiritual and material. As incarnate spirits we are destined for eternal life, even as we live in this material world.

The cross stands at the junction of our identity, both physical and spiritual. The cross also stands at the parting of a Christian view of death and the view of someone who does not know the love and wisdom of our Father in heaven.

This wisdom comes from God rather than from our natural sense life or from the conceptual knowledge of intellectual powers alone.

God infuses this knowledge into our hearts if we are open to receive it. It is heart-knowledge, not just head-knowledge, and it changes darkness into light, absurdity into meaningfulness, death into true life.

Hear again:

> "Unless the grain of wheat falls to the earth and dies, it remains just a grain of wheat. But if it dies, it produces much fruit." *(John 12:24)*

Jesus says, furthermore, that all who want to be his disciples and enter eternal life, will have to begin a "dying" process even in this life. Paradoxically, this dying process is a life of giving, involving some suffering, but will end happily:

> "I tell you truly: you will weep and mourn while the world rejoices; you will grieve for a time, but your grief will be turned to joy. . . . In the same way, you are sad for a time, but I shall see you again; then your hearts will rejoice with a joy no one can take from you." *(John 16:20ff)*

The disciple of Jesus surrenders in faith to a loving Father and gives up inordinate attachments in handing over his life to Jesus, who moves us into a higher existence with him.

Jesus does not trick anyone into following him. He spells out the conditions clearly:

"If a man wishes to come after me, he must deny his very self, take up his cross . . . and begin to follow in my footsteps. Whoever loses his life for my sake will find it." *(Matthew 16:24f)*

The price may seem high — but the reward is incomparable!

# "Do this as a remembrance of me."
**Luke 22:19**

The life-style of Jesus was a paradigm for us to follow. He not only taught us that our lives must be a total giving of ourselves, culminating in death, but he lived that resolve every day of his life on earth. His life challenges us to follow in his footsteps.

Jesus did more. He instituted a way and means which would enable us to give ourselves each day to our loving Father. This channel is a mutual exchange. We give ourselves but we also receive, through this same channel, the help we need to make the total oblation of ourselves.

Let us consider the Mass. Each Eucharistic Celebration is the Church's reoffering of the one eternal offering of Jesus — his life and death to his Father in our name.

He invites us to unite with him in offering this sacrifice. He asks us to bring the gift of ourselves to the altar. The bread and wine represent us and are symbols of our oblation. When we offer food and drink to others, the necessities of life, we are really giving ourselves.

When we present the gift of ourselves to Jesus, he joyfully accepts it and in our name offers it to the Father. We add our gift to his own infinite dimension. Ours is often only half-heartedly given; his makes ours pleasing to the Father.

What a privilege is ours! We are in union with the transcendent, even in our earthly exile.

There is also a reciprocity here. Our Father is not a God outdone in generosity. In response to the oblation of ourselves — all our thoughts, words and actions — he gives us a gift in return, the greatest gift we could imagine: the gift of himself and of his Spirit in the Eucharist of Jesus.

In Holy Communion, Jesus, with his divine life and love, heals our selfishness and strengthens us to be even more generous.

He fills us with his love and motivates and prompts us to give ourselves more consistently and perseveringly. His divine love deserves more total giving of ourselves in response.

This giving of ourselves is what Jesus meant when he bade us: "Do this as a remembrance of me" *(Luke 22:19)*. He encourages us to do what he has done. He gave his whole life to the Father, concerned only with doing the will of the Father.

Jesus was single-hearted in doing so. He assures us that we will be singularly blessed if we, like him, are single-hearted in surrendering ourselves to the Father. "Blessed are the single-hearted for they shall see God" *(Matthew 5:8)*. This single-mindedness is a sure path into heaven.

The whole life of Jesus was an unreserved giving of himself to the Father. The Paschal Mystery was the culmination of this giving.

Jesus was eager to institute the Holy Eucharist. "I have greatly desired to eat this Passover with you before I suffer" *(Luke 22:15)*. The sacrifice, beginning in the Upper Room and terminating on Calvary's heights, was the climax of the giving of himself. Furthermore, he gave it to us as the channel through which we can give ourselves to the Father. Knowing that we would heed his injunction to "do this in remembrance of me" brought him much happiness.

However, Jesus did not want the Eucharist to become a meaningless ritual or a magical formula. He therefore taught us how essential are proper dispositions as we come to the Eucharist. "Authentic worshipers will worship the Father in Spirit and truth. . . . God is Spirit, and those who worship him must worship in Spirit and truth" *(John 4:23f)*.

Earlier, Jesus instructed us in another condition of proper Christian sacrifice:

> "If you bring your gift to the altar and there recall that your brother has anything against you, leave your gift at the altar, go first to be reconciled with your brother, and then come and offer your gift." *(Matthew 5:23f)*

Saint Paul vehemently criticized the Corinthians for improper dispositions in offering the Eucharist *(1 Corinthians 11:17-34)*. Urging generosity in a collection he was taking for the poor, Paul advised:

"He who sows sparingly will reap sparingly, and he who sows bountifully will reap bountifully. Everyone must give according to what he has inwardly decided; not sadly, not grudgingly, for God loves a cheerful giver." *(2 Corinthians 9:6f)*

# 5 Our Own Death

**"It is appointed that men die once, and after death be judged."** Hebrews 9:27

We hear and see much about death. We fear our civilization is disintegrating and that nuclear holocaust is imminent.

The reality of death is all around us. Much of life is a frantic effort to stave off death's finality and its certainty. Every human person must die, yet some ignore this or naively entertain the hope that they will be exempted from this universal law. The moment people are born they begin to die.

Fascination with death in general can avoid any thought about our own personal death. Some contemporary literature deals with the experiences of those who have been "clinically" dead and have returned to life. Such reports tell us that something survives after life and that death cannot be so bad.

There are many faulty attitudes toward death. Hedonists try to enjoy life to the full, believing that death is the end of everything; fatalists accept death as inevitable; agnostics build monuments to preserve their memory; others hope in a series of reincarnations.

Christian attitudes, too, can be faulty. Influenced by dualistic philosophies, some think we are made up of two parts — body and soul — and that death is a violent separation of the two: the body dies but the soul is immortal. According to this view, the soul alone remains waiting for the resurrection to be reunited with the body.

This view is too narrow. The Scriptures tell us that we are made up of body, soul and spirit. Each one of us is a whole person. Our body, soul and spirit develop in this life and this growth continues in the life to come.

Scripture substantiates this theory. To quote just one specific teaching:

> "May the God of peace make you perfect in holiness. May he preserve you whole and entire, spirit, soul and body, irreproachable at the coming of our Lord Jesus Christ." *(1 Thessalonians 5:23)*

According to this scriptural teaching, the "body" ("soma" in Greek) is the whole person, a created personality in the created world. The person is turned outward and becomes more aware of his or her solidarity with the material world.

The "spirit" ("pneuma" in Greek) is the total person turned inward, aware of his or her unique and privileged relationship to God.

The "flesh" ("sarx" in Greek) is the part of man's life disoriented from God.

Death, then, is a disruption or total reorientation of our relationship to the material world through the flesh. Death is the transformation of our animal and vegetative life. However, we remain a whole person and we go into our afterlife as a whole person.

A Christian view is that death is not so much a separation of body and soul as a dying into a new dimension of personal, human life, in which growth continues. With death we come into a deeper consciousness:

> "We have our citizenship in heaven; it is from there that we eagerly await the coming of our Savior, the Lord Jesus Christ. He will give a new form to this lowly body of ours and remake it according to the pattern of his glorified body, by his power to subject everything to himself." *(Philippians 3:20f)*

A summary statement of our Christian belief may be made in these few words:

We believe that when we die we die into eternal life as a whole person. Our consciousness is expanded.

Life on earth consists of dying to self and surrendering more and more in love to God. This process continues in purgatory as well as in heaven. We never exhaust the infinite love of God for us.

With an expanded consciousness and a deeper awareness of God's immense love for us, we become more receptive to the influx of his divine life and love. As we grow in his love in heaven, our joy knows no bounds.

How good is our God and Father!

"Yes, God so loved the world that he gave his only Son, that whoever believes in him may not die but have eternal life." *(John 3:16)*

## "Give, and it shall be given to you."
**Luke 6:38**

Genesis teaches that our first parents had the possibility of reaching their total and complete life with God without the traumatic experience of death. If they had given themselves in a total surrendering love to their Creator and Lord, death as we know it, would not have been necessary. Death is due to sin.

If the first man had not sinned, death would perhaps have been some active movement of grace whereby we would have been translated into the deepest oneness with God and also into a cosmic consciousness of his oneness with the whole created world.

This should not cause us to waste time in idle speculation of how this transition might have taken place. Rather it should lead us into a deeper realization that life is a continuous and complete giving of ourselves to God and his divine will.

We can and ought to give ourselves totally to God in love, not only on our deathbed, but throughout our lives. Each day and each moment afford us opportunities to give ourselves in love to our gracious Father.

We have countless ways of daily making the total oblation of ourselves to God. Recognizing our human limitations, performing the round of daily duties incumbent on our station in life, accepting the condition of our physical well-being and the infirmities of this life — these are some ways of giving ourselves in loving service to the Lord.

Relating to all other persons in our lives with a genuine Christian attitude of love is also a portion of our gift to God each day. Joyfully accepting the comforts or discomforts of the weather and all the expected or unexpected events of daily living are golden opportunities to give ourselves to the Father's plan for us. These are a few ways of dying to self each day and surrendering ourselves in love to God.

Each dying to self opens within us a greater capacity to receive the infilling of God's divine life and love into us.

This is what Jesus meant when he laid down some conditions for our becoming his disciples. He did not try to trick anyone into following him. In his divine wisdom he knew that the "absurdity" of the cross is the royal road to our union with him:

> "Whoever wishes to be my follower must deny his very self, take up his cross each day, and follow in my steps. Whoever would save his life will lose it, and who-

ever loses his life for my sake will save it.
What profit does he show who gains the
whole world and destroys himself in the
process?" *(Luke 9:23ff)*

These conditions sound harsh, but it is in giving that we find greatest joy and satisfaction. If this is true in our human relationships, how much truer it is in the giving of ourselves directly to our loving Father! Love must be our motivating power because love, of its very nature, must give.

Jesus never asks us to do anything which he himself has not already done:

"Such is the case with the Son of Man
who has come, not to be served by others,
but to serve, to give his own life as a ransom for the many." *(Matthew 20:28)*

Using the image of the Good Shepherd, Jesus affirms that he wanted to give his life to redeem us. The motivating power for Jesus and for us must be love:

"There is no greater love than this: to lay
down one's life for one's friends." *(John
15:13)*

Jesus showed us the way to lay down our lives for our loving Father. A daily laying down of our lives will assist us immensely to make the final gift of ourselves in death.

In life we must give ourselves freely and completely to God so that he can be the Lord of our lives. Death is really the climax of choosing either for God or for ourselves.

Jesus told us: "Apart from me you can do nothing" *(John 15:5)*, which is another way of saying that with him we can do all things. Nothing is impossible with God.

Jesus remains with us through the power of his Spirit, so that together we may continue and complete the gift of ourselves to our Father.

Saint Paul holds out this great promise:

"If the Spirit of him who raised Jesus from the dead dwells in you, then he who raised Christ from the dead will bring your mortal bodies to life also, through his Spirit dwelling in you." *(Romans 8:11)*

## "Then we shall see face to face." 1 Corinthians 13:12

At the moment of death we encounter Jesus "face to face" in the clearest and most intimate way. We have met Jesus in so many ways during our earthly sojourn: in our prayers, in the sacraments, in deep awareness of his presence and power.

All of these encounters are enriching, but as Paul says:

> "Now we see indistinctly, as in a mirror; then we shall see face to face." *(1 Corinthians 13:12)*

We will meet Jesus in the overwhelming fullness of his light and love. We know how we long to see someone whom we love and from whom we have been separated for some time. In the first moment of eternity we will see Jesus face to face. We will experience his love, which has been with us all our lives but which we could never comprehend in all its warmth and richness.

Persons who have been pronounced clinically dead and who have been revived seem to agree that they all witnessed a bright light, which did not blind them, and that they enjoyed a tremendous peace and joy. They also tell us that it is impossible to verbalize this "after death" experience.

In spite of all these reassurances and the fact that we are trying to love God with all our hearts, there still lurks within us a fear of death that tempts our faith, hope and love. We experience fears, doubts and misgivings because we see death as the "wages of sin," a punishment for sin.

One reason for this fear lies in the culture in which we live. We evaluate a person by his or her usefulness or productivity. Since this attitude has been ingrained in us, we never consider ourselves worthy of an eternal reward.

Saint Paul tries vehemently to correct this false notion:

"I repeat, it is owing to his favor that salvation is yours through faith. This is not your own doing, it is God's gift; neither is it a reward for anything you have accomplished, so let no one pride himself on it." (Ephesians 2:8f)

Besides all the reassurances that we find in God's Word, we may find comfort in what we are often being told today.

We are told that it is only after apparent death sets in that we are able to make our first completely personal and totally free act of giving ourselves in love to God. During life, some maintain, we are too distracted to make the total gift of ourselves. Now, at the moment of death, we enjoy a full freedom and such a burning love for God that we are able to give ourselves without any reservation.

This is not to be construed as merely giving us a "second chance" after death but, rather, giving us the desire and ability to commit ourselves totally. All this is possible if all through life we have been trying to give ourselves to God by dying to self and surrendering in love to him. Even if our efforts have been self-centered and half-hearted throughout life, we will still be able to make the total gift of ourselves to the Lord at the moment of death.

We may not be able to prove this theory to our satisfaction from Scripture, but it is certainly in conformity with every facet of God's love for us, especially when we recall that God wants to save us more than we can ourselves want it. He loves us with a creating, providing, forgiving, healing, redeeming, enduring love.

How many times has Jesus reminded us that we should not fear? On one occasion he said: "Fear is useless. What is needed is trust" (Mark 5:36). He repeats the admonition not to fear, over and over again.

Who of us can say, even though we do love God as deeply as we can, that when we face death, we will not lose hope in God's mercy? There is mystery surrounding death which affects all of us, saints and sinners alike. We have a powerful and an effective remedy to eradicate this fear in our hearts. Prayerful reflection on the words of Jesus provides hope and consolation, encouragement and fortitude.

Jesus himself reassures us of his great love for us, so overwhelming that he wants us to be with him more than we could want it ourselves:

"No one who comes will I ever reject." *(John 6:37)*

And again:

"Father, all those you gave me I would have in my company where I am, to see this glory of mine which is your gift to me, because of the love you bore me before the world began." *(John 17:24)*

The beloved disciple John assures us further:

"Love has no room for fear; rather, perfect love casts out all fear." *(1 John 4:18)*

Trusting in Jesus' words, what further need have we of reassurance?

# 6 Communion of Saints

## "It was in one Spirit that all of us ... were baptized into one body." 1 Corinthians 12:13

Jesus founded his Church as a community, a family bound together by the bonds of love. In the Upper Room the night before he died, he prayed that his followers might form one body closely united with him. Jesus prayed:

> "That all may be one as you, Father, are in me, and I in you; I pray that they may be one in us, that the world may believe that you sent me." (John 17:21)

Jesus and we, his members, form one Body. Through Baptism we are incorporated into his Body. This oneness with Jesus challenged Saint Paul on the road to Damascus: "Saul, Saul, why do you persecute me?" (Acts 9:4).

Jesus is one with his Body and cannot be separated from it. When Paul was persecuting the early Christians, he was also persecuting Jesus, because of this unity of Jesus with his Body. Saint Paul frequently refers to this, especially in his letter to the Corinthians:

"It was in one Spirit that all of us, whether Jew or Greek, slave or free, were baptized into one body." *(1 Corinthians 12:13)*

Again:

"In his own flesh he abolished the law with its commands and precepts, to create in himself one new man from us who had been two and to make peace, reconciling both of us to God in one body through his cross, which put that enmity to death." *(Ephesians 2:15f)*

Emphatically he wrote to the Galatians: "All are one in Christ Jesus" *(Galatians 3:28)*.

Saint Paul thus continually reminds us that we are one Body with Christ.

Forming one Body of Christ is not like being a card-carrying member of a club or organization. It is much more. Jesus not only exerts influence upon his Body, he is ontologically present in his Body. We are like cells making up the whole Body of Christ.

Paul draws an analogy with our human body:

"The body is one and has many members, but all the members, many though they are, are one body; and so it is with Christ." *(1 Corinthians 12:12)*

We were baptized into Trinitarian life. At that very moment we became members of the most perfect community of boundless love: the Holy Trinity.

God shares his divine life with us, divinizes us. We are temples of the Holy Spirit. Jesus lives with and within us in his risen, glorified life. We are in reality made sons and daughters of our Father.

This is true not only of us, but of all those who are baptized into the Body of Christ. Since we are the adopted children of one loving Father, we are brothers and sisters to one another. We are the family of God.

This truth is especially important in this present age. Our world is becoming more and more a global village. Satellites instantly bring us news of happenings around the world. As we listen to the news and even see on television what is happening, we become a part of all these events. We identify with our brothers and sisters in their joys and triumphs, in their sufferings and sorrows.

Modern technology can help bring us into a spiritual oneness, into a spiritual com-union. By sharing the lot of our brothers and sisters around the world, we are building community.

A loving concern for others builds community, not laws and rules; they are only helpful guidelines. Only love cements people into a oneness.

God is love and in that love we can reach out to others. This is the beginning of community.

This is what the communion of saints is all about. Since we are all incorporated into the Body of Christ, we are closely united to one another in the bonds of love.

We are in communion with our departed loved

ones and with all the angels and saints. We are united with Mary, our Mother, and with Jesus, the Head of his Body.

We are not journeying alone in this land of exile, nor are we only a few mortals laboring to build a community of love here on earth. Rather we are members of the whole Body of Christ.

This consoling truth brings much peace and joy in life's journey.

## "One also is the mediator between God and men." 1 Timothy 2:5

We are invited to be healed of our selfishness, our self-centeredness, and to give ourselves in loving service to God and to our brothers and sisters. This is not easy, nor is it ever fully accomplished. It is a lifelong struggle.

If we do not succeed in making this total oblation of ourselves in this life, there is a further opportunity to continue this effort. Purgatory is a purifying process of dying to self and surrendering in love more totally to God. Likewise, heaven is a continual growth process in our love for God.

We are all members of Christ's Body and of the communion of saints. The saints love us because we are members of the same Body. They pray for us. They bring the healing love of Jesus to all who are broken and in need.

The doctrine of the communion of saints teaches us that all members of the Body of Christ, whether here on earth or in the life after death, remain united — not merely to the Head, who is Jesus, but to one another.

The angels and saints in heaven reach out in

love to all of us. Persons in the purifying process of purgatory also love us and intercede for us.

We on earth, as brothers and sisters, express our loving concern in prayer and intercession.

Mary, our Mother, is the Heart, as it were, of the Body of Jesus, and she is a powerful mediatrix, loving, caring and interceding powerfully for all the members of the Body.

Above all, Jesus our high priest is our Intercessor before our heavenly Father. The power of intercession in the communion of saints is rooted in our incorporation into the Body of Christ. We are intercessors along with him.

Jesus is the Head of his Body. As God's Son his intercession is most powerful, most efficacious:

"God is one.
One also is the mediator between God and men, the man Christ Jesus, who gave himself as a ransom for all." *(1 Timothy 2:5f)*

Jesus is in his glory, continuing his redemptive work among us. He is our eternal high priest continuing to intercede for all of us until we reach our perfect union with him:

"He is always able to save those who approach God through him, since he forever lives to make intercession for them." *(Hebrews 7:25)*

We recognize our own faults and failures, our own wanderings and weaknesses — in brief, the sinfulness which stands between us and our loving Father. Even here there is hope:

> "I am writing this to keep you from sin. But if anyone should sin, we have, in the presence of the Father, Jesus Christ, an intercessor who is just. He is an offering for our sins, and not for our sins only, but for those of the whole world." *(1 John 2:1f)*

Jesus is deeply concerned for us. He wants us to be united with him in heaven, more than we could want it ourselves. Jesus also knows our weak human nature. He knows that we desire to live a sinless life but that our weakness prevails all too often:

> "The desire to do right is there but not the power. What happens is that I do, not the good I will to do, but the evil I do not intend." *(Romans 7:18)*

As with Saint Paul, our privileged position in the Body of Christ and Jesus' forgiving, healing, redemptive, redeeming love move us to cry out:

> "What a wretched man I am! Who can free me from this body under the power of death?" *(Romans 7:24)*

# "You are my children, and you put me back in labor pains until Christ is formed in you." Galatians 4:19

No one was more closely united with Jesus in his sufferings and death than Mary, his Mother. Her life was a complete surrender to God.

Mary made a formal oblation to the Lord at the time of the Annunciation. Her words speak the total self-giving: "I am the servant of the Lord. Let it be done to me as you say" *(Luke 1:38)*. She persevered in her "fiat" from Bethlehem to Calvary and beyond. This total conformity to God's plan prepared her to fulfill the intercessory role to which she was being called.

Even on earth, Mary manifested the power of her intercession. At the wedding feast in Cana, her maternal concern was apparent. Wanting the guests to enjoy the celebration and wanting to save the young married couple embarrassment, she turned with confidence to her Son: "They have no more wine" *(John 2:1ff)*.

Mary understood her Son's loving concern for everyone. Hence she instructed those waiting on table: "Do whatever he tells you."

"Jesus performed this first of his signs at Cana in Galilee" at his Mother's request. This was but the first of his responses to her petitions throughout the centuries.

If Mary is so solicitous about mundane needs, how much greater is her loving concern about our religious needs for our growth and maturation? Jesus wants Mary to ask on our behalf, proving to us her power of intercession.

We believe that Mary now lives in glory with Jesus, intimately united with him and with all members of his Body. During her earthly life Mary gave herself unreservedly to God's will. How much more does she give herself in total love in heaven? This is her glorification.

Mary's glory in heaven, like that of her Son, is not some sort of static reward. Mary's glory is to continue giving herself in loving service to others.

Jesus is our intercessor in heaven. Mary, so closely united with Jesus, also intercedes for us continuously.

Mary gave birth to Jesus. In her glory she wants to form Christ in all the children the Father has given her. Saint Paul could say: "You are my children, and you put me back in labor pains until Christ is formed in you" (Galatians 4:19). How much more strongly can Mary say that to us! Her maternal concern is that we be united with Jesus for all eternity.

This outpouring of her motherly love for each one of us has rightly earned for Mary the title of Mother of the Church. Mary is the Mother of Jesus, the Head of the Church. With Jesus we form one body: the Church. If Mary is the Mother of Jesus and we form one Body with him, she is also truly the Mother of that Body.

The more love we receive from the Father and from others, the more we feel urged to love others. Mary was full of grace. She continued to grow in love as she permitted God's love to make her more open, more present, more concerned about serving others.

Mary stood beneath the cross of her Son on Calvary as he was pouring out every drop of blood for our salvation. Her concern was that not a single drop of that precious blood be spilled in vain. This added great impetus to her powerful intercession for us.

Mary was closely united with Jesus in his death. Let us ask her to "stand" at our deathbed, to take us into her arms and lead us to her Son.

Jesus gave us his Mother to be our very own. We appreciate her powerful intercessory role, and we pray daily:

"Pray for us sinners now and at the hour of our death."

## FOUR

## "From the angel's hand the smoke of the incense went up before God, and with it the prayers of God's people."

**Revelation 8:4**

The space age has made us more aware that we are part of this vast universe. The uncharted areas of outer space remind us of the world of spirits.

Sacred Scripture, in both Testaments, speak to us about angels and the role they play in the economy of our salvation. Since angels belong to the spirit world, there is much mystery surrounding them. Nevertheless, from God's Word we learn something about them. They are the good spirits who worship and serve God.

We have traditionally believed that angels are the channels through which God orders the course of the created world:

> "Bless the Lord, all you his angels, you mighty in strength, who do his bidding, obeying his spoken word." *(Psalm 103:20)*

The angels guide and protect us. They pray for us and with us. They encourage us to the fullness of redemption and to citizenship in heaven. The Church has always maintained that each baptized person enjoys the protection and guidance of an individual angel, which we lovingly call our Guardian Angel.

Jesus warns us:

"See that you never despise one of these little ones. I assure you, their angels in heaven constantly behold my heavenly Father's face." *(Matthew 18:10)*

The angels bring our prayer before God and present them to him along with their own prayer for us. Saint John writes of this vision:

"Another angel came in holding a censer of gold. He took his place at the altar of incense and was given large amounts of incense to deposit on the altar of gold in front of the throne, together with the prayers of all God's holy ones." *(Revelation 8:3)*

Then John continues:

"From the angel's hand the smoke of the incense went up before God, and with it the prayers of God's people." *(Revelation 8:4)*

What consolation it is to know that our prayers are received in heaven by our loving Father and united with the prayers of Jesus and our Mother Mary, in union with the prayers of the angels.

In our daily duties and our meanderings through life, we are never alone. We are accompanied by the angels, under whose care we have been placed.

They guide us through the allurements and enticements of our world and direct us to eternal blessedness, into a union of perfect love with our Father in heaven.

They intercede for us at every moment of the day. How fortunate we are!

## FIVE

**"If one member suffers, all the members suffer with it; if one member is honored, all the members share its joy."** 1 Corinthians 12:26

As Christians we are joined with one another on our way to heaven. We are not travelling alone as if sealed in a space capsule bound heavenward. An individualistic "God-and-me-alone" attitude is unChristian and unreal.

The Church is a family in which we must be concerned about one another. Saint Paul draws an analogy between the Body of Christ and our human body:

> "God has so constructed the body . . . that there may be no dissension in the body, but that all the members may be concerned for one another. If one member suffers, all the members suffer with it; if one member is honored, all the members share its joy." *(1 Corinthians 12:24f)*

We belong to a family — God's family. We are members of a fellowship that is not destroyed by death but, rather, strengthened by it, since the dead are able to love more intensely.

Besides our Church family on earth, we belong to a larger family of God — the communion of saints. We are closely united with those who have gone before us — those in heaven as well as those who may be in the purification state we call purgatory. We call this special family the communion of saints. We form one family, on this earth and in the next, because we all share in the life of Christ:

> "This means that you are strangers and aliens no longer. No, you are fellow citizens of the saints and members of the household of God." *(Ephesians 2:19)*

As the branches and the vine form one plant, nourished by the same life-giving sap, so we are one body, bound together by the divine life shared with us.

The saints in heaven reach out in love to us. They are experiencing God's love in an extraordinary way. Heaven is not a static state. It is a progression, a moving more deeply into God's love. God's love is boundless, limitless, overwhelming, enduring, infinite.

We cannot fathom God's love, nor can we completely absorb it. There is no more possibility of our absorbing all of God's love than a tiny sponge dropped into the ocean has of soaking up the entire sea. Our capacity to receive God's overflowing love is like a thimble trying to retain all the water pouring over Niagara Falls.

The same is true of the saints in heaven. They are sharing deeply in the love of the Lord, but they can never absorb all his love. However, the more love they give away, the more will come to them.

The saints want to share God's love with us. We are the recipients of their love. They have experienced God's love for them far more than we can imagine. As they mediate and share it, they grow more in his infinite love.

They express their love for us by praying continually for us. They know our need for prayer to strengthen and encourage us along life's highway.

The saints walked the same paths we traverse each day. They experienced the temptations, trials and tribulations we encounter. They know we need support, and they are eager to share their love by praying for us. They will continue to intercede for us until we are united with them in heaven.

Saints are good, practical models. We follow models in medicine, business, homemaking, etc. We also are encouraged to imitate the example of those who walked closely with the Lord in this life. By their lifestyle the saints pointed out some particular aspect of Jesus. In imitating the saints who showed us possibilities, we are also imitating Jesus. St. Paul wrote: "I beg you, then, be imitators of me (as I am of Jesus)" *(1 Corinthians 4:16)*.

We have legions of friends with the Lord who pour out their love for us in prayer before God!

## "As generous distributors of God's manifold grace, put your gifts at the service of one another." 1 Peter 4:10

Our friends in purgatory have special intercessory power. Death does not separate them from the Body of Christ. Membership in that privileged Body is everlasting. They are special friends of Jesus and more closely united with him in love which makes the power of their prayers even greater.

These persons have trodden the paths which all of us must walk. They know well the pitfalls we encounter. They once experienced the same difficulties and hardships which we face each day. They also understand our humanness and our weakness. They are very sympathetic with our plight. They long to help us.

Furthermore, purgatory is a process of dying more completely to our selfishness and reaching out in greater love to others.

Jesus atoned for all our sins. He redeemed our sinful human nature. However, Jesus never forces himself upon us. Recall the events on the road to Emmaus after the resurrection. "He acted as if he were going farther. But they pressed him: 'Stay with us. It is nearly evening — the day is practically over.' So he went in to stay with them" *(Luke 24:28ff)*. Notice that Jesus waited for their invitation. Similarly, he wants to share his redemptive love with us more fully, but he waits for us to come with an open mind, heart and hands to receive it.

Sometimes it is difficult for us to know if we are open and receptive to the influx of his divine life and love. We may be clinging to some fault or have some inordinate attachment of which we may not be fully aware. These and many other hindrances prevent us from being receptive to the outpouring of God's love.

Life is a daily dying to our selfishness, surrendering ourselves more completely to God in love. If we have not died totally to ourselves, we are not open to the outpouring of God's love.

The persons in purgatory have not completely died to themselves. The purgation completes this process. One of the most effective means of enabling them to die to self is to reach out in love to others.

As they share their love with others they are emptying themselves so that the Lord may fill them more and more with his life and love. This is why they are so lovingly concerned about praying for us. They express their love for us by praying for us.

All of us are helped by the intercessory power of those in purgatory. If we ask them to pray for a specific intention, we receive their prompt support. It may be we will not receive what we ask for, but we may receive another grace instead. Perhaps a transformation may take place in our desire, or we may be granted the grace of better discernment through their powerful prayers.

Those in purgatory need us, too. They need some recipients to whom they can dispense their love. But they do not wish to reach out in love to us for purely selfish reasons.

They know they are saved. They are experiencing a joy which is far more intense than they ever experienced on earth. They have a burning desire to share this joy with us. They want us to experience this same happiness — hence they are constantly interceding for us that we may die more completely to self and surrender more totally to the outpouring of God's immense love.

The gracious love of those in purgatory deserves our response. We pray they may soon enjoy the eternal bliss prepared for them by a loving Father:

> "Lord of mercy, hear our prayer. May our brothers and sisters whom you called your sons and daughters on earth, enter the kingdom of peace and light, where your saints live in glory."

## SEVEN

## "Pray constantly and attentively for all in the holy company." Ephesians 6:18

We can and do support one another in prayer. We can intercede for each other. We can thank God for the gift of one another.

Jesus leads us into prayer by his frequent instruction and by his own example. He urges us to intercede and pray for one another's needs. On one occasion he asked us to pray that all people might receive the Good News of God's love for them:

> "The harvest is rich but the workers are few; therefore ask the harvest-master to send workers to his harvest." *(Luke 10:2)*

Jesus here implies that our intercession will bring many blessings to our brothers and sisters in need.

Jesus also taught us by his own example how important and how necessary it is for us to pray with and for one another. Jesus had his own special prayer team who supported him in his ministry. He took Peter, John and James with him to pray as he raised the daughter of Jairus to life

*(Luke 8:51).* He invited them to pray with him on Mount Tabor when he needed strength and support to accept his mission of suffering *(Luke 9:28ff).*

At another crucial time in his life Jesus felt the need to be supported by the loving presence and prayers of his three favorite disciples. When he entered the Garden of Gethsemane to begin his dreadful passion he took along Peter and Zebedee's two sons and went into the inner Garden where he asked them to pray with him. How plaintive are Jesus' words when they failed him: "So you could not stay awake with me for even an hour?" *(Matthew 26:40ff).*

The apostles frequently instructed the early Christians to pray for one another:

> "Pray constantly and attentively for all in the holy company." *(Ephesians 6:18)*

> "I urge that petitions, prayers, intercessions, and thanksgiving be offered for all men, especially for kings and those in authority, that we may be able to lead undisturbed and tranquil lives in perfect piety and dignity. Prayer of this kind is good, and God our Savior is pleased with it, for he wants all men to be saved and come to know the truth." *(1 Timothy 2:1ff)*

> "Pray for one another, that you may find healing. The fervent petition of a holy man is powerful indeed." *(James 5:16)*

Praying with and for another has continued down through the centuries. Christians have the duty to reach out in loving concern to all their brothers and sisters, living or dead.

The Church prays for the conversion of sinners, for the spread of the Good News and for all those in need, whether the need be physical, spiritual or psychological.

From the days of the catacombs to our own day, the Church has always prayed for those who have died. Jewish tradition in the century before the coming of Christ held that it was "a holy and pious thought" to pray for the dead *(2 Maccabees 12:38ff)*. By praying for the dead we continue our love for them and our gratitude to God for the gift of each one of them.

Intercessory prayers culminate in the Eucharistic Celebration. In fact, the Church suggests special Masses for the needs of ourselves and our brothers and sisters, here on earth or in the life hereafter.

Prayers offered in Mass are especially powerful. At Mass we place our petitions into the hands of Jesus, our mediator before the Father. Jesus first unites our prayers to his own prayer, adding an infinite value to our prayers.

Our prayers with and for one another are an ideal way of fulfilling Jesus' injunction:

> "Love one another. Such as my love has been for you, so must your love be for each other." *(John 13:34)*

Praying for another person is the most powerful and effective way of establishing a deep personal relationship with that person. Our loving concern expressed in prayer binds us into a oneness in the Body of Christ, because his divine life flows into all of us:

"Pray perseveringly, be attentive to prayer, and pray in the spirit of thanksgiving." *(Colossians 4:2)*

## EIGHT

## "You, then, are the body of Christ. Every one of you is a member of it."
**1 Corinthians 12:27**

The title of a popular song a few years ago wisely admonished: "Count Your Blessings!" Count especially the many blessings which come to us from our incorporation into the Communion of Saints.

Mary our Mother, the angels, the saints, and even our loved ones who have left this earth need us. Startling? God's divine plans are mysterious.

The members of the Communion of Saints who have preceded us in death really do need us. They need to share the immense love of God burning within them by reaching out in loving service to all of us here in our earthly existence. They also long to extend their love to all those still in need of healing and purification after their death.

The greatest power we have is the love which causes us to forget ourselves in order to love another unselfishly. Like us all, Mary and the saints are the adopted sons and daughters of the Father. They are filled with his limitless love. This love urges them to share their joy with others. Their tremendous love of God impels them to bring his love to others.

Mary in her glory, the angels, the saints already glorified in heaven, those departed persons who are still waiting for full admission into heaven, and all of us here on earth — this is the family of God. We are all members of the Church, whether it be the Church triumphant, the Church suffering or the Church militant. We are the Church under the headship of Jesus, bound together by one common love.

This is the kingdom which Jesus founded and into which we have been received, thanks to his boundless love for us. Jesus prayed that we might be one, closely united with him and with all our brothers and sisters, living or dead:

> "That all may be one as you, Father, are in me, and I in you; I pray that they may be one in us, that the world may believe that you sent me." *(John 17:21)*

Our oneness is achieved by his indwelling within us. His divine life animates his whole Body, on earth and in heaven:

> "There is but one body and one Spirit, just as there is but one hope given all of you by your call. There is one Lord, one faith, one baptism; one God and Father of all, who is over all, and works through all, and is in all." *(Ephesians 4:4ff)*

Thus we are one family, with God as our Father, under the headship of Jesus our brother, vivified and united by the love of the Holy Spirit.

What hope and reassurance, what peace and what joy we have in the realization that others in heaven and on earth are helping us by their prayers! What satisfaction and happiness it brings us to know that we can help others immeasurably by praying for them.

What a blessed privilege is ours to be a member of the Body of Christ:

> "You, however, are a chosen race, a royal priesthood, a holy nation, a people he claims for his own to proclaim the glorious works, of the One who called you from darkness into his marvelous light."
> *(1 Peter 2:9)*

No greater dignity could be ours. God has committed to us the fullness of his love.

Heaven begins right here, right now!

We are fortunate to be members of that elite family: the Communion of Saints.

# **7** Purgatory

## "He made atonement for the dead that they might be freed from this sin."
**2 Maccabees 12:46**

We have been taught that after death there are three states, one of which awaits us: heaven, hell or purgatory. Let us prayerfully consider the state of purgatory.

What do we know and what does the Church teach about purgatory?

Two passages in Scripture are frequently quoted in support of the doctrine on purgatory. In 2 Maccabees 12:38-46, Judas sent two thousand silver drachmas to Jerusalem to provide for an expiatory sacrifice:

> "If he did this with a view to the splendid reward that awaits those who had gone to rest in godliness, it was a holy and pious thought. Thus he made atonement for the dead that they might be freed from this sin." *(2 Maccabees 12:45f)*

To the Corinthians Paul wrote:

> "The work of each will be made clear . . . fire will test the quality of each man's

work. . . . If a man's building burns, he will suffer loss. He himself will be saved but only as one fleeing through fire." *(1 Corinthians 3:13ff)*

There is no explicit doctrine on this state of purgation in the Old or New Testament, yet these texts of Scripture support our belief in purgatory.

Furthermore, we know more about the doctrine of purgatory from the universal practice of the Church in offering prayers, good works, alms and Masses for the deceased members of the Body of Christ.

We substantiate what we believe about purgatory from Sacred Scripture, by the writings of the Fathers, the liturgical services, the lives of the saints and certain private revelations and visions.

From all of these we conclude that there is a healing for the dead brought about by the prayers of individuals and of the Church, especially in the Eucharistic Liturgy.

Today we are becoming more aware that purgatory is not so much a punishment due to sin which needs satisfaction, as it is a kind of necessary healing. It is a further maturing of the individual after death.

God is not a vindictive God who heaps punishment upon us for our sinfulness. On the contrary, God wants us to die to self, to grow and mature, to be healed of anything which prevents us from being receptive to the outpouring of his infinite love upon us. If God were a vindictive God, how could he say:

"It is I, I, who wipe out, for my own sake, your offenses; your sins I remember no more"? *(Isaiah 43:25)*

We are the cause of our own punishment. In life we have made our own free choices. Many of these were not in harmony with God's will. With the gift of free will we are able to say "no" to God's love for us. God's love is limitless. Sin closes us to the influx of that gracious love.

Death expands our consciousness. Death brings us into a new and deeper awareness of the goodness of God and his infinite love for us. When we contemplate his boundless love for us we see more clearly our own lack of generous response to his love, our indifference to his will of preference, or even our failure to respond at all to his love.

This awareness is the source of our punishment. We begin to understand how ungrateful we have been throughout our life. We comprehend more clearly how our pride, our spirit of independence and our self-centeredness have prevented us from opening to the great love God has wanted to pour out upon us.

The Father proved his great love for us by giving us his Son Jesus and the Holy Spirit dwelling with us and within us, operative within us at every moment of our lives. We begin to see ourselves as we really are. As we experience God's goodness and love, shame and sorrow fill our hearts.

Peace and pain can coexist within us. We experience great joy because of the presence of

God's enduring love. We are sorrowful because of our self-centeredness; we have failed to respond to God's gracious love.

Now we understand the malice of sin more realistically. We realize more keenly what our personal sins have done to our crucified Jesus. We see how our hatred, our bitterness, our resentment, our selfishness, our indifference toward our brothers and sisters have contributed to the sufferings of the Body of Christ.

As our vision clears in this way, the words of Jesus at the Last Judgment come to mind:

> "I assure you, as often as you neglected to do it to one of these least ones, you neglected to do it to me." *(Matthew 25:45)*

As we contemplate Jesus' whole message at the Last Judgment, sorrow for our indifference to those in need will well up in our hearts. This will cause us pain, but it will also be the beginning of a great healing.

Purgatory may be painful, but it is also a process of healing. After this healing, full union with the Father is assured.

# "Yes, God so loved the world that he gave his only son." John 3:16

In our life on earth the Holy Spirit has made of us his temples. He fills us with his divine love. "The love of God has been poured out in our hearts through the Holy Spirit who has been given to us" *(Romans 5:5)*.

This love dwelling within us brings us to a genuine sorrow for our own sinfulness. It also fills us with an intense love for God because he continues to love us just as we are. How much more will the Holy Spirit be operative if we need purgatorial healing?

In the Good News the Holy Spirit reveals to us that:

> "For our sakes God made him who did not know sin, to be sin, so that in him we might become the very holiness of God."
> *(2 Corinthians 5:21)*

This is what the dynamic, operative, redemptive love of Jesus is accomplishing in us at this very moment.

"Yes, God so loved the world that he gave his

only Son" *(John 3:16)*. And: "There is no greater love than this: to lay down one's life for one's friends" *(John 15:13)*. Jesus came to prove the reliability of God's love.

This love, more than anything else, will be the healing therapy we need to uproot our selfishness.

One of the purifying effects of purgatory will be to bring us to a deeper knowledge and appreciation of God's love, not only for us personally but for all other human beings.

We will experience more fully God's unique love for us personally. We will also see how God gives himself and his love to us through others. God's love comes to us through the love of Jesus for us, through our Mother Mary, through the angels and saints. His love comes to us especially through the loving family and friends he has given us.

As healing takes place in us, our love yearns to reach out to our loved ones with greater intensity. At that moment any self-centeredness will rise up and cause us pain as we recognize our lack of love in the past, as well as our agonizing inability to love them as we ought.

Prayer is an expression of love. It is our way of communicating love. When we pray for those in purgatory, they are aided by our prayers. When we beseech God for them, we are expressing our love for them and there is much healing power in that prayer.

Love has inherent healing power. God cannot

93

be outdone in generosity. When we pray for the departed that they may be healed, we ourselves are healed. So good is God!

When we pray for those in purgatory, our love expressed in prayer calls them out of their isolation and loneliness into a newfound identity. They realize that they are not alone; they are loved. The healing power of love builds community, a oneness, a togetherness in loving union with Jesus and with one another.

In his "Confessions," Saint Augustine writes touchingly of his own mother's death. In her dying request to her priestly son she begged: "Lay this body anywhere at all; the care of it must not trouble you. This only I ask of you, that you remember me at the altar of the Lord wherever you are." *(IX chapter XI)*

The Council of Trent summarizes an ancient tradition of praying for the deceased in these words: "The souls detained there (purgatory) are helped by the suffrages of the faithful and principally by the acceptable Sacrifice of the Altar."

Jesus is always dying mystically on behalf of each person. His intercessory power is limitless, since he is the Son of God interceding for his brothers and sisters. His prayer is for all of us, whether we are in the Church Militant on earth, the Church Suffering in purgatory or the Church Triumphant in heaven.

Through her liturgy the Church extends to all the faithful departed the sacrifice of Christ which takes away sins. She prays that God may pardon and purify the deceased of all their sins.

The Church is one. Christ is the Head; we are the members. We enjoy the love extended to us and, in turn, we can touch others with our love.

## THREE

## "The fervent petition of a holy man is powerful indeed." James 5:16

At some time all of us must have experienced the intercessory power of those in the process of purification. Perhaps we have laid an urgent petition before them and discovered how quickly our request was granted in some way, even if not specifically as we asked.

The persons in purgatory are being purified and healed of their self-centeredness. During this process they are free and eager to exercise the newfound love which the Holy Spirit has poured into their hearts. Their prayerful love reaches out to touch their own loved ones, those who have provided healing love for them, and also to those who are in great spiritual need of God's love.

It is true that the angels and saints have a greater power of intercession because they are filled with God's presence and purified of all selfishness. Nevertheless, those persons in purgatory have a God-given love and loyalty toward their own loved ones and toward all those with whom they lived and worked while on earth.

As these persons reach out in love to God by

interceding for their loved ones and acquaintances, they are truly becoming more and more receptive to the infilling of God's divine life and love within themselves. As they empty themselves they are enlarging the capacity to receive a greater influx of divine love.

Healing comes from the uprooting of self-centeredness. As those persons in purgatory love those in need, they are eradicating any selfishness in their own lives. Jesus pointed this out when he said: "There is no greater love than this: to lay down one's life for one's friends" (John 15:13).

The Father loves us with an immutable love. Jesus told us he loves us with that same love. "As the Father has loved me, so I have loved you" (John 15:9). He proved his love by laying down his life for us on the cross. In turn, the Holy Spirit pours out his love upon us, his disciples, even upon those in the state of purification. "This is how all will know you for my disciples: your love for one another" (John 13:35).

Those persons in the state of purgation have experienced the kenotic love of God for them. In response, they give. The only genuine manifestation of the new level of healing they have attained through the love they have received is to give their love to those who need it.

In a certain sense we are a gift to these souls, since we provide them with an outlet for the love they have received. They, in turn, are gifts to us, as they communicate their love in praying for us.

A person undergoing the therapy of purgation

suffers affliction and torment. Paradoxically, however, this is always accompanied by a deep joy and peace.

An analogy might help us to understand this mystery. A young bride suffers both torment and joy at leaving her family and loved ones to begin a new home with her bridegroom in a distant city. Her experience is an admixture of both sorrow and joy.

Saint Catherine of Genoa described the joy of those undergoing the healing therapy of purgatory:

> "I believe no happiness can be found worthy to be compared with that of a soul in Purgatory except that of the saints in Paradise; and day by day this happiness grows as God flows into these souls, more and more as the hindrance to his entrance is consumed. Sin's rust is the hindrance, and the fire burns the rust away so that more and more the soul opens itself up to the divine inflowing. . . . As the rust lessens and the soul is opened up to the divine ray, happiness grows; until the time be accomplished the one wanes and the other waxes. . . . Never can the souls say these pains are pains, so contented are they with God's ordaining with which, in pure charity, their will is united."

Love is often accompanied by pain. However, the joy of loving far outweighs the pain. The joy of those in purgatory outdistances the suffering they endure.

## FOUR

# "Do not be surprised, beloved, that a trial by fire is occurring in your midst."
**1 Peter 4:12**

Have you ever wondered just *where* purgatory is? When we speak of heaven, almost instinctively we look upward, and we think of hell as below. When we think of purgatory, we are left a little confused.

Like heaven and hell, purgatory is not a place. If purgatory is not a vindictive punishment meted out by an avenging God to extract satisfaction for the violation of his laws, then there is no need for a purgatory in time and space.

Purgatory is a condition or state which a person fashions during his or her lifetime on earth. Purgatory is a state in which we live in harmonious or disharmonious relationships. If our relationships are peaceful and loving, the purgatory we fashion is less severe. On the other hand, if we have lived a life of selfishness and refused to reach out in love, our purgatory will be proportionate because our need for healing will be greater.

Purgatory, then, is a state where healing takes

place. Purifying love and healing can take place even in this life.

Another question which arises in our minds is the possibility of fire in this state of healing.

Again, we may say that purgatory is a process of maturing and becoming a whole person. We grow, mature and become a real disciple of Jesus by overcoming past bad habits, correcting ignorance, letting go of resentments, dealing with our unforgiveness and all the other roadblocks that we have wittingly or unwittingly permitted to direct our course through life.

This purifying process can be painful. We often speak of being purified by fire. The sacred writers often mention fire as a purifying element. Here are a couple of references:

> "As the crucible tests silver and the furnace gold, so a man is tested by the praise he receives." *(Proverbs 27:21)*

And:

> "For in fire gold is tested, and worthy men in the crucible of humiliation." *(Sir 2:5)*

Metaphorically, we speak of the fire of purgatory because it is a state of purification. The purifying effect of purgatory is similar to the purifying power of fire in melting away the dross from pure metal.

Perhaps the agonizing purification of the mystics comes closer to the idea of such a "fire." Saint John of the Cross has described well the agonizing purifications which some mystics must undergo, especially the purification of the spirit. Saint John describes it as: "A living flame of love that tenderly wounds my soul in its deepest center."

This is perhaps the closest description of the sufferings of those persons in purgatory. It is easily understood why the term "fire" has been used to designate the suffering of those being purified.

In summary, we may conclude that purgatory should not be thought of as a state of terrifying, penal punishment. Rather it should be seen as a state where those close to God are being healed of anything which stands in the way of a deep, personal, loving relationship with him.

Futhermore, those persons who are being healed in purgatory are loving intercessors toward us here on earth and also toward those with them in purgatory who need their healing presence and love.

Purgatory is real. It is as real as all of us in this life and in the life to come who have not yet surrendered ourselves completely to Jesus.

Purgatory is painful. It is joyful. It is learning to die to self. In this process of dying to self, we are experiencing new levels of love in the risen Savior.

Purgatory is a vital part of heaven. It is the antechamber leading us into the fullness of happiness, peace and joy as we are embraced in the loving arms of our Father.

# **8** Heaven

**"We groan while we are here, even as we yearn to have our heavenly habitation envelop us." 2 Corinthians 5:2**

What is heaven like? Have we asked ourselves or others this question? In prayer or flights of fancy, have we tried to picture to ourselves what heaven must be like?

A young boy was returning home from Mass with his mother. Both of them had just heard a moving homily about the joys of heaven. On the way home the mother was extolling the happiness they could anticipate in heaven. Her son seemed pensive. When the mother asked what was troubling him, he asked very honestly: "Mother, if I am good and go to heaven, do you think they will let me go out sometimes and play with the little devils?"

Saint Paul, quoting the prophet Isaiah (64:3), writes:

> "Eye has not seen, ear has not heard, nor has it so much as dawned on man what God has prepared for those who love him." *(1 Corinthians 2:9)*

Paul's imagination, though vivid, could find no words to describe heaven. However, we do know that heaven is our life with God, our loving Father. And what do we know about God?

God created the whole universe and everything in it. He created people and endowed them with the understanding to cooperate with him in bringing the universe into a higher state of perfection.

Our loving Father is not a powerful Creator who brought the whole universe into existence and then retired to his heaven to be only a transcendent God, far removed from his handiwork. No, he is also an immanent God who lives with and in his creatures. "In him we live and move and have our being" *(Acts 17:28)*.

God is omnipresent. He fills the heavens and the earth. "Where can I go from your spirit? From your presence where can I flee?" *(Psalms 139:7)*.

God is present everywhere because he is love. God is present not only in his gifts as an expression of his love, but he is present in actual union. He gives himself totally to us, living with us and within us.

What an awesome mystery is God's infinite condescension and his humility in desiring to give himself to us and to share his very life with us!

God not only communicates himself through all his gifts of creation, but he is present in all the handiwork of his creation. He is the sustaining, energizing and directing force in all creation.

God is present in us. We are created and

103

destined for a oneness with Jesus and through him with the Father and the Holy Spirit:

"God is love, and he who abides in love, abides in God, and God in him." (1 John 4:16)

This overwhelming mystery was revealed to us by Jesus. God created us because he loves us. In his love for each one of us, he destined us for love by permitting us to participate in his own divine life:

"Eternal life is this:
to know you, the only true God, and him whom you have sent, Jesus Christ." (John 17:3)

Jesus teaches us that God's purpose in creating us is that we may become members of his family and that we may share in his divine life. Through our Baptism he adopts us as his sons and daughters. We are incorporated into his family. We become brothers and sisters to one another, because we share a common life, his own divine life and love:

"I solemnly assure you, no one can enter into God's kingdom without being begotten of water and Spirit." (John 3:5)

The height of God's becoming present to us and of his self-giving to us is the Incarnation. He gave us his only-begotten Son, who is the way that leads to eternal life. Jesus is the God-man,

God made flesh. He is God's preferred way of communicating himself to us. Jesus sanctifies us by his Holy Spirit, who shares divine life with us. Jesus lives with us and within us in his risen, glorified, exalted life:

"Praised be the God and Father of our Lord Jesus Christ, who has bestowed on us in Christ every spiritual blessing in the heavens! God chose us in him before the world began, to be holy and blameless in his sight, to be full of love; he likewise predestined us through Jesus Christ to be his adopted sons — such was his will and pleasure — that all might praise the glorious favor he has bestowed on us in his beloved." *(Ephesians 1:3ff)*

# "Inherit the kingdom prepared for you from the creation of the world." Matthew 25:34

"The kingdom of God" (or "heavenly rule") is used frequently in Sacred Scripture and quoted by Jesus. God's incomprehensible desire to share his own nature and the Trinitarian life with us is what Scripture means by the "kingdom of God."

Within each one of us is an insatiable longing for fulfillment of all our desires, especially the desire to be loved. Anthropologists have proven that all races and cultures have professed a belief in some sort of unending happiness and a fulfillment of all human desires for those who live according to certain standards.

This goal for us is heaven, our homeland, life with our Father.

Our belief in heaven is much more than an unending life after death. God's Word in Sacred Scripture tells us something of heaven. But even here there is much mystery and much left unsaid. Jesus himself did not reveal much about heaven. He was primarily concerned in teaching us how to live our mortal lives, so as to reach our eternal union with him.

It was not Jesus' mission on earth to describe eternity, but rather to announce the Good News of the "reign of God." Nevertheless, the implications of Jesus' teaching, the constant tradition of the Church and the insights of the saints and mystics reveal much about heaven to us.

In the Old Testament the Jews refer to heaven as the dwelling place of God, from which he sends us his blessings. Human sin closed our access to heaven or paradise. The chosen people were waiting expectantly for God's saving power to open the gates of heaven once again so that God would pour down his blessings abundantly upon them. God's covenant with man would be completed when man returned to God in heaven.

We do know that heaven is the unending loving presence of God. Jesus always walked in that presence of his heavenly Father while on earth. He was one with the Father. Did he not say: "The Father and I are one" *(John 10:30)*? This oneness suffused his whole humanity. His glory was his oneness with the Father.

Jesus turned inward to find the Father at the core of his being:

"Believe me that I am in the Father and the Father is in me." *(John 14:11)*

This hidden glory that came from the indwelling of the Father burst forth in the transfiguration of Jesus on Mount Tabor. The splendor which radiated from Jesus in the transfiguration manifests to us that Jesus was always in heaven while on earth, because he was always one with the Father and with the Spirit. This is what we call the beatific vision.

Heaven is not a static state where we gaze on God's splendor in all its perfection. The risen Jesus gives us some deeper insights into heaven. It is not a vacation or an honorable retirement, but a dynamic, operative living with the Holy Trinity. It is a state of continual growth.

Scripture and our own personal experiences tell us that we have been made by God to live in a community of loving persons who call us into an ever-increasing self-sacrificing love.

We have been baptized into a community of perfect love — the Holy Trinity. This is the kingdom of God announced by Jesus. Jesus promised a loving, indwelling, communitarian relationship between us, himself and his heavenly Father:

> "Anyone who loves me will be true to my word, and my Father will love him; we will come to him and make our dwelling place with him." (John 14:23)

Jesus also promised to send us the Holy Spirit, who would abide with us and within us (John 14:26, 15:26 and 16:7f). We are destined for community. The Holy Spirit has made us his very own temples. He leads us to the Son: "No one can say: 'Jesus is Lord,' except in the Holy Spirit" (1 Corinthians 12:3). And Jesus leads us to the Father: "No one comes to the Father but through me" (John 14:6).

In heaven we will be bathed, enveloped, saturated with God's love for us. We will be like a sponge saturated by the ocean which surrounds and permeates it. Just as the sponge cannot absorb the immense water of the ocean, neither can we ever soak up the infinite love of God for us. This is the growth process of heaven.

Heaven is knowing God as he is: "Face to face" *(1 Corinthians 13:12)*. We will be gifted with intuitive knowledge which will help us understand the infinite love of the Trinity. We will also know how we can continue to be human while growing in God's life.

The beatific vision, then, is a dynamic process of continued growth in love of God and love of neighbor. Heaven is a state of continuous growth toward God and toward all our brothers and sisters. We want more and more to reach out in loving service to other human beings.

In heaven we contemplate the self-giving love of the Trinity within us and acknowledge the Trinitarian life in other persons. We love and are loved with an incomprehensible, ever-increasing love. We are fully possessed by God, continually overwhelmed by his beauty and goodness, and yet always thirsting for more, even as we are filled to perfect contentment. We seek and continue to find more. Each one of us knows God and is loved by him in the most intimate way possible. We are loved in a way that no one in creation is or ever will be. That is what heaven is all about.

## THREE

## "We have come to know and to believe in the love God has for us." 1 John 4:16

Heaven is our union with God and with one another in perfect love. We will constantly be growing in love and happiness.

Even in this life our consciousness can be widened. In heaven this expansion is ever-increasing as we come to know and understand the Holy Trinity intuitively.

Reflect on this in this way. It is difficult to read small print in a dimly lit room. In sunlight we see more clearly. If we think of sunshine as the presence of God, then we can readily understand growth of consciousness in heaven.

Another very important dimension to our life in heaven is our ability to love more intensely. In heaven we know all those we knew and loved on earth. We know all the saints and great people we admired on earth. There are no strangers in heaven. We delight in one another's perfections and in our mutual love.

As our love grows in heaven we praise and thank God for his constant, infinite goodness. We better understand how faithful and loving he has been throughout our whole life on earth. Here in this land of exile we know God's faithfulness by faith:

> "We continue to be confident. We know that while we dwell in the body we are away from the Lord. We walk by faith, not by sight. I repeat, we are full of confidence and would much rather be away from the body and at home with the Lord. This being so, we make it our aim to please him whether we are with him or away from him." *(2 Corinthians 5:6ff)*

In heaven we have intuitive knowledge of God's limitless, enduring love for us, and we thank him with all the choirs of angels and saints.

We rejoice in the greater knowledge of what God has done for us in our individual lives. We want to share this knowledge with all the other persons in heaven, united with us in the Body of Christ.

We want to praise God for himself. His creative love is ongoing. With the psalmist we sing:

> "The heavens declare the glory of God, and the firmament proclaims his handiwork." *(Psalm 19:2)*

We praise the Blessed Trinity especially for all the self-giving in the creation of the angels, saints and all intelligent beings.

We praise God for the humanity of Jesus and for the gift of Mary and her total self-giving, through the fullness of his grace and love given her. Nor do we forget the fidelity of the angels, especially our guardian angels.

In heaven we praise God for our family and the gift of our parents, brothers, sisters, relatives and all our dear friends who did so very much for us. Without their love we might never have reached our eternal home with them. One of the joys of heaven is sharing with them for all eternity not only their past generous love, but the continuous, limitless new ways of loving us.

Husbands and wives grow together in greater love for each other, as together they praise God in that love. Parents are again united with their children, and their mutual love grows for each other as they discover God and his many ways of loving:

> "No one has ever seen God. Yet if we love one another God dwells in us, and his love is brought to perfection in us." *(1 John 4:12)*

In heaven fear is gone forever. It is replaced by love. We no longer experience misunderstanding, criticism, jealousy, resentment or any of the aggressive attacks of others. All these unhappy experiences are replaced by a gentle, warm, Christlike love. This gentleness enables us to witness and receive God's presence shining through every human and angelic being we meet in heaven.

The God in us embraces the God in our neighbor, and we respond with the excitement of discovering the infinite, unspeakable beauty of God in others. The fear of rejection is gone. We are loved and accepted by everyone.

We are one in Christ. There are no strangers, no enemies. We are all brothers and sisters in Christ. We are not only members of a family, but the Body of Christ:

> "How shall I make a return to the Lord for all the good he has done for me?" *(Psalm 116:12)*

## FOUR

**"In my Father's house there are many dwelling places; otherwise, how could I have told you that I was going to prepare a place for you?"** John 14:2

We have an insatiable curiosity about what heaven must be like. When we turn to the Scriptures and search the Word of God, we may be disappointed at the dearth of information about the exact nature of our life in heaven.

In the Bible there are many references to life hereafter as an eternal union of love with the triune God. In fact, the entire Word of God is geared to this truth. The way and means we must follow to reach this state of eternal bliss are clearly spelled out.

The Old Testament refers to heaven as the dwelling place of God. From this place he sends out his blessings.

After man had sinned, heaven (paradise) was closed. The chosen people waited expectantly for the coming of the Messiah who would open once again the gates of heaven. When this was accomplished, God would again pour down his blessings abundantly upon them, and they would be living a utopian life as the chosen people.

The Jews also believed that when God's covenant with man was completed, man would return to God in heaven and live happily with him.

The Old Testament or Hebrew Scriptures do not give specific information about heaven.

Nor do we find enough information in the New Testament to satisfy our curiosity. As we have said, Jesus taught us how to live his Way of Life so that we might eventually be with him in heaven. However, he gave us little information about the nature of our life with him in heaven.

The New Testament writers use a variety of images:

"life eternal" *(John 12:25);*
"the kingdom prepared for you from the creation of the world" *(Matthew 25:34);* "the wedding day of the Lamb *(Revelation 19:7);* "the great feast" *(Revelation 19:17);* "the heavenly Jerusalem" *(Hebrews 12:22);* "the holy city Jerusalem coming down out of heaven from God" *(Revelation 21:10);* "God's dwelling place among men" *(Revelation 21:3).*

Heaven is also described as the "place" from which Jesus came and to which we will someday go to be with him. These descriptions of heaven are only symbolic, as is the imagery of heaven found in the Book of Revelation. They are attempts to capture some of the mystery. As we have seen, neither Isaiah nor Paul pretended to grasp what our heavenly home will be like.

Paul said simply:

> "Eye has not seen, ear has not heard, nor has it so much as dawned on man what God has prepared for those who love him." *(1 Corinthians 2:9)*

When we think about heaven or speak about it, we automatically look upward. Though our concepts are bound by time and space, heaven is not a place, and it is difficult to image it as a state.

Heaven is a state of being whole, glorified persons along with the angels and saints, and with the glorified humanity of Jesus and Mary. It is being "together" and being for each other.

The "how" and the "where" are God's mysteries. Before raising Lazarus to life, Jesus declared:

> "I am the resurrection and the life: whoever believes in me, though he should die, will come to life; and whoever is alive and believes in me will never die. Do you believe this?" *(John 11:25f)*

Jesus was testing Martha's faith by asking this question.

Our finite minds simply cannot grasp or visualize what life in heaven is like. This requires faith and trust. Jesus leads us into that kind of expectant faith:

> "Do not let your hearts be troubled. Have faith in God and faith in me. In my Father's house there are many dwelling

116

places; otherwise, how could I have told you that I was going to prepare a place for you?"

Then Jesus gave us his solemn promise:

"I am indeed going to prepare a place for you, and then I shall come back to take you with me, that where I am you also may be." *(John 14:1ff)*

## FIVE

## "See, I make all things new!" Revelation 21:5

Heaven is the ultimate experience of human life and faith. It is the climax of stepping out in faith and accepting Jesus as our Savior. Our faith began with Baptism. At that moment the Holy Spirit made of us his special temples. With his dynamic divine presence within us, our resurrection already began.

Heaven is the continuation of the life we began on earth, where we learned to love. We reached out in love to our gracious Abba in heaven. This relationship called us into being and sustained us throughout our earthly journey. It will not only be present in heaven but will continue to call us to new levels of being for all eternity. Heaven is the beginning of full life.

When we became the temples of the Holy Spirit, he shared his divine life with us. It was implanted in us like a tiny seed. We can be compared to a tree. Our roots must be firmly established in the ground if we are to survive the winds and storms of daily living. Our arms must reach out confidently toward heaven from which the sunshine of God's divine life nourishes, strengthens and cheers us. The winds and the storms strengthen us as we withstand their onslaughts.

The Liturgy calls heaven "eternal rest." This is merely an attempt to convey to us the perfect peace, contentment and security in knowing that heaven will last forever.

Security and peace are precious to us because we spend so much time coping with meaningless, frantic work and the contrived "relaxations" of modern life.

Heaven is really living at last. It is continual growth in knowledge and love, an endless expanding of our whole being while enjoying tremendous peace and contentment.

Heaven is the continued process of knowing and loving God as the source of our life and everything we have and are. Heaven is resting in God as the ultimate good. It is reaching out in concern and loving service. Speaking of our final destiny, Saint Paul says: "Christ is everything in all of you" *(Colossians 3:11)*.

Scripture pictures heaven by images of activity and celebration, of feasts, joyous worship of praise and thanksgiving, of sumptuous banquets and rewards for our service of God.

Servants who have been faithful in little things during life on earth will enjoy all the good things of the Lord.

In his visions, as related to us in the Book of Revelation, John writes:

"I saw new heavens and a new earth. The former earth had passed away, and the sea was no longer. I also saw a new Jerusalem, the holy city, coming down out of heaven from God, beautiful as a bride prepared to meet her husband." *(Revelation 21:1ff)*

Even the inspired writer was unable to verbalize what heaven is like. His vision gives us hope and encouragement here in our land of sojourn.

By contemplating God's infinite love for us, we hear him telling us that heaven has already begun here on earth, as he comes to live with us and within us.

In his Word he assures us of his immanence and his abiding with us, filling us with his love, inspiring and motivating us, encouraging and strengthening us, carrying us in the palm of his hand:

"This is God's dwelling among men. He shall dwell with them and they shall be his people and he shall be their God who is always with them. He shall wipe every tear from their eyes, and there shall be no more death or mourning, crying out or pain, for the former world has passed away. . . . See, I make all things new!" *(Revelation 21:3ff)*

All this and heaven, too!

# Epilogue

## Awaiting Our Own Resurrection

Jesus came into the world to teach us a way of life which would lead us, after our own resurrection, into an eternal union with him, the Father and the Holy Spirit.

One of the most effective ways to prepare for our own resurrection is to spend some time each day with the Lord listening to his Word. His Word has the power to inspire us to live his Way of Life, the power to transform our minds and hearts. Above all, in his Word he assures us of his boundless love for us and challenges us to respond in love to the outpouring of his tender love for each of us.

Our daily date with the Lord is the surest, safest road to resurrection. During the quiet time spent in prayer, the Lord will open new vistas on our journey heavenward and lead us on to distant horizons in peace and joy. These experiences in prayer will help us form a rich, personal relationship with Jesus, our travelling companion throughout life.

# CALL

Jesus calls us to be his friends, his followers. Our resurrection was initiated at Baptism. Jesus came to live with us and in us through the power of the Holy Spirit. His indwelling empowers us to respond to his call.

When we were baptized into the Trinitarian life, we were like a seed planted in the Church. We are to grow to full maturity as children of God and living members of the Body of Christ.

Paul gives us this reassurance:

"In baptism you were not only buried with him but also raised to life with him because you believed in the power of God who raised him from the dead." *(Colossians 2:12)*

Speaking of the Father's plan for us, Paul again reminds us of our call to resurrection:

"He brought us to life with Christ when we were dead in sin. By this favor you were saved. Both with and in Christ Jesus he raised us up and gave us a place in the heavens." *(Ephesians 2:5-6)*

## CONVERSION

Our own resurrection, then, began with our Baptism, when we were given a share, a participation in the Trinitarian life. The new life is increased each time we "put on Christ" by dying to our self-centeredness and rising to a new oneness in him. Our human weakness hinders this new life from reaching its fullness until the time of our final resurrection.

In our prayer Jesus invites us to come with him to the Mount of Beatitudes. There, in the Sermon on the Mount, he sets forth his Way of Life. Jesus gives us the norms and guidelines which will lead us to final resurrection.

He not only teaches us his Way but points also to his own lifestyle as a model, an ideal for our imitation. Prayerfully listening to Jesus' teaching will give us new insights into him as a Person who loves us so dearly.

Jesus came not only to die for us, but also to rise from the dead to create a new resurrected life which he shares with us. To help us enter into this living experience of God as our loving Father, Jesus teaches us the necessity of a conversion, a turning toward God.

Jesus teaches us how to turn away from our self-absorption and turn totally to God. Such a conversion is a God-given gift to those who earnestly go out of self to seek him. It consists not so much of certain devotional practices or programs of apostolic action as, rather and primarily, of a change of heart and mind so as to effect an inner conversion.

Jesus tells us we must be reborn of the Spirit he will send:

"I solemnly assure you, no one can see the reign of God unless he is begotten from above. . . . No one can enter into God's kingdom without being begotten of water and Spirit." *(John 3:4 and 5)*

Our Christian concept of resurrection embraces what happened to Jesus after his death on the cross and then his glorious rising from the dead. This will happen to each one of us after our earthly death.

Speaking to our hearts in the quiet prayer of listening, Jesus will show us how to nurture and care for the seed of divine life which has been implanted in us.

Our conversion or conditioning is a transforming process which will take place in the fruitful years of our Christian living. In faith, hope and love we must yield to the transforming and divinizing power of God's Spirit.

Jesus states this fact picturesquely:

"I solemnly assure you, unless the grain of wheat falls to the earth and dies, it remains just a grain of wheat. But if it dies, it produces much fruit." *(John 12:24)*

The seed of divine life and love which we received in our Baptism grows, develops and matures from the spring planting through its summer growth, yielding a rich harvest.

The winter of life may be the time of death, but it is by no means the end. Winter is but the threshold of spring. For the followers of Jesus, it is an eternal spring.

# COMMITMENT

In our daily prayer we arrive at the third stage of our spiritual journey toward resurrection: commitment. Before making our commitment, Jesus invites us to come with him to the Upper Room. There we sit with him as he speaks his parting words to us in his Last Discourse. His farewell message is one of great encouragement and expectation.

He assures us once again that as the Father loves him, so he loves us. He reminds us of his abiding presence as the source of the "living waters" of his divine life which animates, energizes and sustains us.

Jesus also promises to send his Holy Spirit to enlighten, guide, strengthen and sanctify us as we journey through the maze of daily living.

In this final discourse, Jesus teaches us another valuable lesson. How nobly he rises above all the hatred, rejection and plotting against him! He does not indulge in self-pity. His only concern is for us. Thus he reveals another facet of his divine personality: his loving concern for others. He bids us to imitate him in this aspect, in our own ministries.

Our prayer will elicit within us a great desire to respond to his immense love. As we experience the outpouring of God's love for us, we will desire to respond to that love by giving ourselves graciously to him.

As conversion takes place in us, God gifts us

with a special enlightenment, provided we open up to receive his Word as the earth opens to receive the seed. This enlightenment shows us the meaninglessness of worldly, self-centered values. It does not stop there. It also shows us the sheer joy of surrendering to God's holy will in all our decisions.

This enlightenment continues to create in us new depths of awareness of our own spiritual poverty which will lead us to a yearning to live God's will of preference. This is commitment.

The Bible recounts many stories of men and women who committed themselves totally to the Lord — from Abraham to Moses, from the Prophets and the Apostles on down to Paul and beyond.

Mary's unreserved commitment highlights all the others. In a few brief recorded words, Mary made a commitment which was total and eternal:

"I am the servant of the Lord. Let it be done to me as you say." *(Luke 1:38)*

Jesus pointed to his own lifestyle as an example for us to follow: "What I just did was to give you an example: as I have done, so you must do" *(John 13:15)*.

When Jesus promised us the gift of himself in the Holy Eucharist, he also assured us that we would not be rejected by him, because his Father wants our salvation. Jesus was able to make this promise because his life of dedication was pleasing to the Father. Listen to his own words:

126

"All that the Father gives me shall come to me; no one who comes will I ever reject, because it is not to do my own will that I have come down from heaven, but to do the will of him who sent me." *(John 6:37f)*

Jesus' whole earthly sojourn was a total compliance with the Father's will. He often reminded us of this fact so that we, too, might persevere in our commitment.

In the Garden of Gethsemane, Jesus was able to make the greatest of all human decisions because he had committed himself exclusively to doing the Father's will. Let the implication of his resignation touch our hearts as we listen:

"Father, if it is your will, take this cup from me; yet not my will but yours be done." *(Luke 22:42)*

The next day, Jesus gave the total gift of himself to the Father from his deathbed on the cross:

"Father, into your hands I commend my spirit." *(Luke 23:46)*

Surely Jesus has shown us the way. His infinite love for us makes our commitment possible, and even joyous.

We are able to make our commitment because Jesus is always with us. He never leaves us. He is not only walking with us in this life, but he will be with us at the moment of our death and will lead us into resurrection. For he said:

"I am the resurrection and the life: whoever believes in me, though he should die, will come to life; and whoever is alive and believes in me will never die." *(John 11:25f)*

"COME, LORD JESUS!" *(Revelation 22:20).*

A brochure listing other books by the author may be obtained from

**Living Flame Press**
Locust Valley, New York 11560